Written by:
Andy Chambers,
Pete Haines & Graham McNeill

Cover Art:
Adrian Smith

Internal Art:
Alex Boyd, Paul Dainton,
Jes Goodwin & Karl Kopinski

Graphic Design
John Blanche & Stefan Kopinski

Colour Production
Mark Raynor & Adrian Wood

Miniatures Designers
Tim Adcock, Juan Diaz,
Jes Goodwin, Mark Harrison,
Trish Morrison, Brian Nelson,
Alan Perry & Michael Perry

Miniatures Painters
Martin Footitt, Neil Green,
Dave Thomas, Tammy Haye,
Keith Robertson, Chris Smart,
& Kirsten Williams

Model & Scenery Makers: Dave Andrews and Mark Jones

*Special thanks to Gav Thorpe, Marc Gascoigne and the
Ancient and Honourable Order of Tech Priests*

PRODUCED BY GAMES WORKSHOP

British Cataloguing-in-Publication Data. A catalogue record for this book is available from the British Library.

Games Workshop World Wide Web site: http://www.games-workshop.com

Second Printing

UK	**US**	**Canada**	**Australia**	**Japan**
Games Workshop Ltd., Willow Rd, Lenton, Nottingham, NG7 2WS	Games Workshop Inc., 6721 Baymeadow Drive, Glen Burnie, Maryland 21060-6401	2679 Bristol Circle, Unit 3, Oakville, Ontario, L6H 6Z8	Games Workshop, 23 Liverpool Street, Ingleburn NSW 2565	Games Workshop Ltd., Willow Rd, Lenton, Nottingham, NG7 2WS

Greetings, Commander, to this sacred text that will help you to further the Greater Good by guiding you in collecting, painting and gaming with a Tau force in the Warhammer 40,000 game. The Tau way of war is efficient and deadly, combining the hi-tech wargear and weapons of the Tau with the aggression and close combat prowess of their mercenary allies, the Kroot. A Tau commander recognises the skills and abilities of all those under his command and uses them to fearsome effect.

THE TAU

The alien race known as the Tau inhabit an area of space near the eastern fringe of the galaxy and are a young, dynamic race, with highly advanced weaponry and technology. Though less than two thousand years old, their fledgling empire is rapidly expanding into space and encountering all the elder races of the galaxy. In galactic terms their empire is small, based around a densely packed globular cluster of stars, which enables the Tau to travel between them without many of the dangers normally associated with warp travel. The Tau empire also encompasses several alien races who have been subsumed into the empire voluntarily or whose services are bought through trade agreements.

Tau civilisation is based around a rigid system of castes, each relating to the four elements of nature – fire, water, air and earth – which dictate a Tau's particular role within their society, be it warrior, bureaucrat, pilot or worker. Their rulers form a mysterious fifth caste, translated as the Ethereals, who bind the other castes together. The Tau empire is underpinned by the concept that it is only right and noble for the individual to set their own desires aside to work together for the greater good of the empire. Overall, they're very good at it too.

Unlike most alien races which Humanity has encountered, the Tau are not overtly hostile, though they will fight fiercely to protect those territories they have claimed as their own. The sheer dynamism of the Tau is pushing them further into occupied areas of the galaxy and this has inevitably brought them into conflict with both Humans and other alien races.

WHY COLLECT A TAU ARMY?

The Tau are a very stylish and powerful army with many specialised troops at their disposal. Their main strength lies in the different types of battlesuit equipped warriors. These warriors are hardened veterans and their battlesuits are capable of mounting a fearsome array of firepower. Combined with their exceptional armour protection, this makes them very difficult to take out with most troopers' basic weapons. If you're looking for an army that can pack a heavy punch while being able to soak up the enemy's return fire, then the Tau are the force for you. Tau technology is highly advanced with many exciting devices and upgrades with which you can equip the battlesuits to further enhance their ability to deal death.

Tau Fire warriors are courageous fighters with solid leaders, and if a member of the Ethereal caste accompanies them, their confidence and self belief will keep them fighting in the face of insurmountable odds. The Tau dislike close combat, preferring to destroy their enemies at long range with hi-tech weaponry as they are neither particularly strong or tough. When the fighting is likely to get close and bloody, the Tau can call upon allies in the shape of the Kroot. The Kroot are ferocious carnivores employed as mercenaries and are capable of holding their own against most opponents.

The ongoing expansion of the Tau empire ensures that they are frequently encroaching into other races' territories and border disputes are quick to flare up on the frontiers. Tau space borders on many Ork-held systems and several Imperial sectors. Craftworlds have passed through their space and the first tendrils of the Tyranid Hive Fleets are approaching. This means that it is perfectly possible to fight any opponent in the Warhammer 40,000 universe. Whatever army your opponent has, you can fight him with no qualms about whether or not such a battle would ever arise.

A fully-painted Tau army looks very striking on the tabletop and suits painters who want the best of both worlds. On the one hand you have the clean, elegant lines and bright colours of the Tau Fire warriors in their battlesuits and grav-tanks, while on the other you have the Kroot, with their barbaric, feral feel and large areas of flesh to colour. Even very basic painting techniques will quickly produce a battle ready force, giving you the chance to quickly and easily build a playable army and begin to expand the frontiers of the glorious Tau empire. May the Ethereals guide you, Commander.

Shas'O Vior'la Kais, Fire warrior Commander, watched dispassionately as the Gue'la began the long trek up the hillside. Their crude, armoured vehicles lumbered forwards on clanking metal tracks, dismounted warriors advancing before them. Kais felt sorry that he had to do this; the Gue'la could not know the folly of this attack. The Tau had claimed this world as their own. Its use had been decided, its first colonists already allocated from members of the Fio caste. It was as indisputable as a sunrise. The Gue'la already had an outpost on this world and Kais was in the process of removing them. The Ethereals had decreed this but, with typical Gue'la stubborness, they had refused to bow before the inevitable.

As the Gue'la advance continued, Kais' superior vision could make out the forms of his Pathfinders concealed in the tall grass before them. Already their markerlights were pinpointing the noisy vehicles for his more powerful weapons. He turned to one of his bodyguards, a smooth helmeted warrior in a pale coloured battlesuit.

"Do you see the armoured beasts, Shas'vre?" asked Kais formally.

"Yes, Commander. This should present no significant problem. The Shas'la have marked them clearly for the Broadside battlesuit squad's railguns."

The Commander of the Fire warriors nodded.

"Then you may begin, Shas'vre," he intoned softly. The warrior nodded reverently and spoke quietly into his helmet mike. Almost as soon as he did so, three of the Gue'la vehicles exploded and lurched sideways, black smoke pouring from neat holes in their front and rear armour. The hypervelocity slugs of the rail guns were too fast even for Kais' augmented vision, leaving only searing afterimages where the friction of their passing had ignited the air.

The Gue'la scattered, stunned at the death of the iron machines. It was unfortunate that they would die, but to stand in the way of the Tau's destiny was to invite death. It could not be helped.

A flurry of gunfire flared from a concealed position to the left of a smoking tank. The Gue'la in front of the vehicle fell, cut to ribbons by the Pathfinders' weapons. As soon as the Gue'la fell, the Tau were on the move. More Gue'la moved around the tank, firing their weapons at where they believed his warriors to be. Their shots hit nothing, the Pathfinders having long since relocated to new positions.

Then, from out of the smoke, came the Kroot. Tall and lithe with powerful muscles corded around their arms, they charged into the mass of Gue'la. Blasts from their vicious rifles pitched several to the ground and Kais knew that they were the lucky ones. They attacked with a high, ululating battle cry, spinning their rifles and slamming the thick blades on the butts of their guns into Gue'la flesh. Their Shaper beheaded a Gue'la with one sweep of his blade and howled, shaking the long quills on the back of his head free in triumph as the rest of the enemy fled before him. The Battlesuit teams now moved down the hillside, firing into the disordered Gue'la troops. Kais' brow wrinkled in distaste as he saw several of the Kroot warriors stoop to take bites from the fallen Gue'la bodies. To defeat one's enemy in combat was one thing, but to eat his flesh… he shivered in disgust. The Kroot were useful and Kais valued their strength, but he had hoped that the continued contact they were having with the Tau would have purged them of some of their baser instincts by now.

He turned away from the feeding Kroot and spoke again to his bodyguard. "You may contact the Kor'vre and inform him that he may begin landing the Fio'la immediately. This world is ours now."

OVERVIEW OF THE TAU

Far from Terra, in the eastern reaches of the galaxy, lies the empire of the Tau. Though not extensive it encompasses a region of space some three hundred light years in diameter, with the Tau home world at its centre, and nearly a hundred settled worlds. A number of these worlds are home to alien races which are either subservient to the Tau or whose services are bought. The Tau are a young race, barely six thousand years old, yet they are highly advanced technologically and their empire is expanding rapidly, pushing further into space with growing self-confidence.

DISCOVERY

The first Imperial contact with the Tau race came roughly six thousand years ago in 789.M35, when the Adeptus Mechanicus Explorator vessel, *Land's Vision*, discovered and categorised what is now their home world of T'au. Initial investigations revealed the planet to be dry and arid with few lush areas and an abundance of oceanic, aerial and terrestrial xenomorphs. The first Adeptus Mechanicus teams to explore the planet noted that the savannah dwelling aliens had mastered the use of primitive weapons and discovered fire, but nothing of worth was perceived in their continued existence and the world was earmarked for routine cleansing and colonisation. Seeding ships were despatched to begin the colonisation of Tau but, before they arrived, freak warp storms of unimaginable fury engulfed them and, despite the presence of highly skilled navigators and captains, every vessel in the colony fleet was lost. Rather than simply blowing themselves out, the warp storms continued to make space travel impossible for light years in all directions, and many whispered that this was a sign the planet was cursed. In any case, the cares of the Imperium soon turned to more pressing concerns.

The 361st High Lord of the Administratum, Goge Vandire had proved to be a paranoid megalomaniac and led the Imperium into one of the bloodiest periods in its war-torn history, the Age of Apostasy. This is not the place to speak of Vandire's Reign of Blood, suffice to say that he was eventually overthrown and stability restored to the Imperium when Sebastian Thor was elected Ecclesiarch. The rebuilding of the Imperium was to take many hundreds of years and, while this work was under way, the warp storms cutting T'au off from Imperial scrutiny continued to rage, concealing the nascent development of the Tau race.

ADVANCED EVOLUTION

On the forgotten backwater of T'au, the species first catalogued by the Adeptus Mechanicus grew bigger and stronger, some plains tribes migrating further and further afield as hunting grounds grew scarcer in response to the increasing population. As the centuries passed, each branch of the Tau began developing in their own way, displaying a unique talent for rapidly adapting to their chosen environment. High on isolated mountain peaks, Tau soared on thermals, rising up from the hot plains on thin, membranous wings, and found plentiful employment amongst the other Tau as messengers and scouts. Those whose migrations had carried them to lush river valleys began establishing well-constructed farming communities, developing their metallurgical, toolmaking and mining skills to create the first Tau settlements. Others realised that different communities could produce what they could not and negotiated trade agreements between the disparate tribes, recognising the inherent value in each others' skills. The larger Tau who remained on the plains grew stronger still, becoming skilful and aggressive hunters. They took what they wanted and if they had to fight in honourable battle to get it, so much the better.

For some unknown reason, Technological innovation was at a more accelerated pace than would normally be expected for a newly emergent race. The Tau who had begun building the first communities quickly escalated to use fortresses and simple blackpowder weapons to defend their settlements from marauding tribes of plains dwellers allied with the Tau of the air. Trade routes were cut and the Tau who negotiated between the various tribes were attacked to prevent alliances from being formed. Soon vast intertribal wars ravaged the main continent, with Tau tribes turning on each other in savage battles utilising primitive firearms. The wars dragged on for many years, thousands dying on every side and with no end to the slaughter in sight. Squalid conditions caused by the fighting and a lack of fresh food and water allowed a virulent plague to spread rapidly across the continent until more Tau were dying of disease than were being killed in battle. As the savagery of the fighting escalated, it seemed as though the Tau race would surely extinguish itself in the fires of its own barbarity.

THE ETHEREALS

The Tau now entered their darkest age, when the entire race was being destroyed by war and disease. As the 37th millennium drew to a close, many strange portents and omens were observed such as flickering lights in the night sky and half-glimpsed figures in the mountains. Many believed that these were signs that they were living in the last days, that extinction was nigh. 'The Ethereals of Fio'taun' is one of the foremost legends amongst the Tau and tells of how their race was pulled back from the brink of annihilation.

The legend tells that on a mountain plateau called Fio'taun, an alliance of plains dwellers and air Tau laid siege to the mightiest fortress-city of the builder Tau. Nearly seven thousand beings dwelt in the great citadel and, in vain, the traders attempted to negotiate with the plains warriors. Their blood was afire and they would brook no settlement save that delivered at the end of a rifle. For five seasons the cannons of Fio'taun held the attackers at bay, but supplies were low and disease was rife within the city walls. As night fell upon another bloody day's fighting, the leaders within Fio'taun prayed for a miracle. Little did they know that on this night their prayers would be answered.

Emerging from the darkness, a Tau of unusual appearance walked into the besiegers' camp, asking to see the army's commander. He was softly spoken, yet it is said that he had an undeniable authority and the sentries to whom he had announced himself found themselves compelled to escort him to their leader. At the same time, within the walls of Fio'taun, a similar individual presented himself to the guards of the fortress. How he had penetrated the defences of the city he would not say, all he asked was that he be allowed to speak to the castellan of the fortress. Again, his request could not be denied and he was permitted an audience with the city's leader. Within the hour, the fortress gates were opened, the stranger guiding the citadel's leaders towards the torchlit camp of their attackers.

As the gates opened, they were met by a party from their enemy, led by a figure who was the stranger's twin in all respects. The two newcomers called themselves Ethereals and bade the others sit. Beneath a maiden moon of purest white, they began to speak, explaining that the talents of each of the tribes could be harnessed. They spoke of a Greater Good that could be achieved if they would put aside their warlike ways and work together. The two strangers talked through the night, their words carrying great power, and as the sun crested the horizon, a truce had been agreed between the warring factions.

Fio'taun was just the beginning. Soon, more of the Ethereals emerged and the message of peace and greater good began to spread to every corner of the globe, the battles slowly dying out as the new philosophy took hold. Within the space of a year, the wars were over and the Tau flourished like never before. Well-constructed towns and cities sprang up throughout the continent, commerce routes were re-established by the traders and communications maintained by the air Tau. The warriors of the plains were the hardest to convince that this was the way forward, but as they saw the civilised wonders being created by the other castes,

they finally agreed to the Ethereals' entreaties that they become honour bound defenders of the Tau. It was decreed that from that day forth each of the tribes would be known by the element that most befitted its role in the greater good. The builders and artisans would be the Earth caste, the traders the Water caste, the messengers and scouts would become the Air caste while the warriors of the plains would be known as the Fire caste. Having saved the Tau from a slow racial extinction, the Ethereals were revered with the utmost devotion by the other castes, binding and guiding them as they looked towards the future with a new found sense of hope.

DYNAMIC EXPANSION

The next thousand years saw an almost unprecedented renaissance of scientific discovery and cultural and philosophical advancement. Working together for the greater good became the cornerstone of Tau society, the ultimate ideal to strive for. It enabled the Tau to fully utilise each caste's talents and allowed them to send their first rockets into space. The Air caste were heavily involved in the early exploration of space and, within a short period of time, orbital communities were established and the colonisation of the nearest moon, , was well underway. With orbital docks, larger vessels could be constructed and Tau ships ventured further and further afield, with communities developing on almost every viable moon, world and planetoid within reach. Air caste astrogators produced the first stellar maps of nearby celestial bodies, revealing that their home world lay within a globular cluster of densely packed stars. The attendant risks of novae and supernovae prompted further expansion and the Earth caste began the construction of even larger colony ships.

The expansion of the Tau empire continued at an explosive rate, with the Tau making contact with a number of alien races and, despite the destruction of several ships, the empire continued to advance. Many less advanced alien races were incorporated within its borders and most of these willingly became part of the Tau empire. The Orks were a notable exception to this and the Tau fought many battles with the Greenskins before finally abandoning their attempts to subsume them into the empire. After the successful navigation of a warp rift, the Ethereals and Air caste worked to refine the technique of travelling through warp space but, without the specialised mutation of the Navigator gene, their colony ships could only make short 'hops' into warp space, skimming the edges of the immaterium. With the tightly packed nature of the Tau empire, this did not prove to be a problem and protected them from many of the inherent dangers of warp travel.

Given their limited exposure to the warp, the Tau found it difficult to comprehend the hallucinogenic effects it had on other races and the terrible threat it could represent to psykers. Such talents were a mystery to the Tau as they had no psychic abilities whatsoever, their minds barely even registering in the warp at all.

Soon the Tau empire stretched over a little more than three hundred light years and incorporated eight heavily settled systems known as septs. These formed the hub of the empire, with colonies outposts and waypoints established throughout Tau space.

At the frontiers of Tau space, on the world of Pech, traders with an escort of Fire caste warriors encountered a Kroot enclave and fought alongside them in a battle against Ork raiders. In the Kroot, the Tau recognised a strength they could harness, and soon Kroot warspheres began to appear with more regularity in Tau expeditionary forces. While the thought of the Kroots' cannibalistic tendencies repulsed the Tau, they valued and respected their strength as warriors, perhaps believing that continued contact with the Tau would eventually show the Kroot the error of their ways.

IMPERIAL CONTACT

With such rapid expansion of their empire, it was only a matter of time until Tau colony ships entered Imperial controlled space. System defence ships stationed at Devlan in the Ultima Segmentum detected the arrival of an alien vessel which did not halt at the designated checkpoints, and immediately attacked it. Unprepared for such an aggressive response, the Tau ship fled, but was unable to make good its escape as Imperial Navy ships summoned by the planetary governor destroyed it in an engagement at the system's edge. An Imperial investigation was launched into this technologically advanced race when Adeptus Mechanicus Genetors discovered that genetic samples taken from the corpses on the alien ship matched those of the primitive xenos discovered six thousand years ago by *Land's Vision*.

Further, less violent contact with the Tau was made by Rogue Traders and merchants exploring the darkness of the eastern fringes. Far from the guiding light of the Astronomican, warp travel so far in the galactic east was treacherous and word of such contact was slow to filter back to the Administratum. Members of the Water caste had established trade agreements with Imperial worlds on the frontier and exchanges of goods and technology were common. Alarmed by the threat of alien contamination, the Administratum readied a suitable response and almost a century later, the Damocles crusade smashed into Tau space, destroying several outlying settlements and pushing deep into the Tau empire. But when the Imperial fleet reached the sept of Dal'yth, the crusade ground to a bloody

stalemate as the formidable numbers and high technology of the Tau and their Kroot allies thwarted every attempt to capture the system. After many months of terrible fighting, with nothing gained on either side, Imperial commanders eventually agreed to requests from the Water caste for peace talks. The negotiations were successful and the Imperial fleet withdrew from Tau space, partially in response to the negligible chance of victory, but also due to the impending approach of Hive Fleet Behemoth. As the fleet withdrew, Tau forces, one of which was led by the infamous Commander Farsight, followed in its wake and retook their lost worlds, assimilating groups of Human deserters and renegades in the process.

The Tau empire continues to expand its borders, pushing ever further into space and establishing colonies on every world capable of sustaining life. However, a new threat has arisen in the form of Tyranid splinter fleets from Hive Fleet Kraken and the Battle of Ichar IV. Attacks from the Tyranids have fallen upon several Tau worlds and the terrible danger these voracious super-predators represent has quickly been realised by the Ethereals. As contact is lost with yet more colonies, the Tau empire girds itself for war.

THE CASTE SYSTEM

As decreed by the Ethereals, Tau society is divided into four castes, each based on one of the four elements of nature. Tau are born into their caste and breeding between the castes is forbidden by the Ethereals. By use of the caste system, not only are the Tau performing the most basic form of genetic engineering, but they also reinforce the individual's belief that they have a position to fill in the empire and that their efforts are rewarded. The four castes are as follows:

Fire – The Fire caste are the warriors of the Tau. It is the duty of these warriors to protect the other castes. Centuries of selective breeding has led to the Fire caste being the biggest and strongest of the Tau. The Fire warriors are strongly motivated by a strict code of honour in battle, but

they are not mindless thugs. They see ranged combat as preferable to the somewhat brutal affair of close combat, as they are not naturally equipped for such fights, preferring to use advanced weaponry rather than brute force to win battles. A warrior starts life as a young line trooper, a Shas'la, and after surviving four years 'on the line' they must take their first Trial by Fire. If they survive this ordeal then they are fit to don the full battlesuit. If they survive a further four years, they take the second Trial and successful participants become Shas'ui. A veteran who manages to survive yet another four years becomes eligible to take part in a third Trial if he wishes and, if he is still alive by the end, will become a Commander, or Shas'el. Commanders who survive four years are allowed to retire from active service, join the council of advisors and play a greater part in Tau politics. Other than death, this is the only way to leave the Tau military.

Earth – The Earth caste are the artisans and labourers of the Tau. It is they who build the machines, erect the dwellings and provide the food for the rest of society. Without the Earth caste, the farms would not produce, the factories would sit idle and the work would remain undone. None of the other castes would be able to live without their continued existence. Engineers and scientists beyond compare, the Earth caste are responsible for the maintenance of Tau technology but, unlike the Tech-priests of the Imperium, they fully understand the workings of their machines and are capable of more than simply reproducing ancient designs.

Water – Water is the element that can be found in all living things, flowing continuously to allow life to function. So it is that Water caste members are bureaucrats, politicians, negotiators and administrators. They are the merchants and diplomats, moving in and around the other castes to make sure that society functions smoothly. Water caste members often accompany Tau expeditionary forces to negotiate safe transit through alien systems and smooth the passage of Tau merchants and colonists.

Air – The Air caste members were traditionally messengers and couriers but now, with the march of technology, they are the Tau equivalent to the Imperial Navy. They are pilots and spaceship crews, transporting goods and warriors to where they are needed. They are the unseen force that can lay waste to towns and cities, bombarding them from orbit. Air caste members live almost entirely off-world, except for pilots of atmospheric craft (although frequently they live in orbital stations). They are the invisible caste, normally unseen but essential nonetheless.

The Ethereals – The Tau word 'Aun' translates variously as the Celestial or Ethereal caste, and originates from the mysterious individuals who united the disparate Tau tribes. These are the rulers of the Tau empire, headed by a council of the wisest Ethereals. They are advised by members of the highest families within the different castes, but have ultimate sovereignty over all the Tau. It is speculated that they exert some kind of pheromone based or latent psychic control over the other castes, as loyalty to the Ethereals is absolute and unswerving. If an Ethereal were of such a mind, he could order another Tau to kill himself and would be obeyed immediately. The Adeptus Mechanicus and Adeptus Arbites are very interested in this aspect of Tau culture…

A TAU'CYR AMONG THE KROOT

LETTERS FROM PECH

BY FIO'UI BORK'AN ULYR'RA

To Fio'la Bork'an Vashrun Ka'la

When I was told that there was spare capacity in the message boat I could not resist writing to you, my sister. I trust you prosper as Tau shall.

The greatness of the Empire is truly a marvel. For the last three kai'rotaas my Ta'lissera has been on Pech, home world to the barbaric Kroot. Fear not sister, their penchant for savage behaviour is thoroughly held in check by their desire to be part of our great Tau Empire. They allow us to go where we will and readily submit to medical inspection so we can better understand them and guide them forward.

I have to tell you that if our preliminary research is substantiated then our estimation of the Kroot will have to be revised considerably.

Our most remarkable finding is that the Kroot are capable of selective mutation. We now have evidence that the life form we refer to as Kroot is merely the most successful of a wide range of divergent species with the same genetic root.

Their form can evolve significantly over the span of four or five generations. While for most species evolution is a journey so gradual that it cannot be witnessed by mortals, I have seen Kroot returning from service with the Shas'ar'tol which have developed an ability to withstand chlorine atmosphere in the course of a few tau'cyr. Major changes I would suggest are possible, but require a greater exposure to the source of the mutation, possibly over several generations.

In this case the source of mutation is their diet. As we have known for some time, the Kroot feed on the flesh of the dead, an unwholesome and primitive practice which many hoped we could persuade them to abandon. In fact this practice is the source of the Kroots' greatest strength and their largest potential contribution to the Empire.

The Kroot are organised into family groups, which we called kindreds. The elder of this group, termed a Shaper, is apparently able to analyse the content of its gut and extract from it characteristics that might be of use to the Kroot genetic code. This task is apparently performed intuitively, but demonstrates a mastery that the finest minds of Bork'an would struggle to conceptualise. Once a characteristic of their prey is identified then the Shaper will direct members of the family group to consume this particular prey animal. Breeding is then controlled to ensure that those who have absorbed the chosen genetic morsel fix it as part of their own DNA.

From the standpoint of pure survival we have a carrion eater that, faced with a more dominant life form, can absorb its characteristics within a very short time. It is likely that the Kroot have used this technique extensively as within every broad category of fauna on Pech there is an example which is 99% Kroot.

The Kroot have evolved from avians, that much is clear, although whether this original form was similar to the Kroothawk is speculation. They still retain beaks and a light bone structure. Life abounds on Pech's primary continent, so the proto-Kroot could always feed. But for their genetic quirk, they would have remained in this state while other life forms became the dominant species. The cause of the anomaly is unknown but at some point the Kroot genetic code began to mutate. As I hope you have learned, sister, the bulk of normal DNA contains no data but merely serves to divide the data that does exist. The Kroots' mutation turned this space into a blank slate for retention of new genetic data. The mutation is not random in its working; instead the Kroot seem to be able to make choices. The more complex the DNA of the food, the more likely the Kroot will absorb something useful. Successful adaptations thrived, others died out. The overall effect was a rapidly accelerated evolutionary program which left the Kroot the dominant species on Pech long before such a situation should have been possible.

The Kroot brain is unusual insofar that it is a combination of cerebral hemispheres and clusters of ganglia. The ganglia run the length of their crests and are very efficient at interpreting sensory information, a feature which, combined with their superb senses, makes the Kroot very difficult to hide from. In this regard the ganglia are similar in function to the Tau thalamus. They have two cerebral hemispheres, one behind the other. The front hemisphere controls logic and memory and is considerably more developed than the other hemisphere, which governs imagination and creativity. Kroot interpret what they perceive and react accordingly, with little emotional clutter. The rear hemisphere is another mutation; it controls their inventiveness and imagination and has a very limited capacity. Whilst it is more pronounced in some Kroot kindreds, this limits the Kroots' creativity considerably, with the consequence that they have gone about as far technologically as they are likely to go without the help of a more sophisticated people.

The Kroot have little capacity for further mutation without seriously destabilising their DNA. They cannot therefore acquire every advanced trait they encounter or their variety will end, trapped in a single form that is a genetic dead end. Kroot Hounds and Krootox are examples of this error being made in the past. Kroot history is littered with these evolutionary cul-de-sacs, although their rapid development is testament to its effectiveness.

The Kroot digestive system is capable of breaking down virtually any organic substance to a pure energy form which they retain in organs, called nymunes, spread throughout the body. The stored energy can be used to maintain the Kroot during a lengthy hibernation period. The Kroot, as carrion eaters, are quite content to wait out their prey, and can initiate a state of hibernation at will during which their metabolism slows to a halt.

The Kroot are a bizarre mixture of evolutionary quirks. Unable to urinate or defecate, they have probably the most efficient digestive system I have ever examined. Virtually nothing they consume is wasted although some undigestable materials are regurgitated, and chemicals synthesised from their food are released as thick viscous sweat. I know it is unfitting for a Fio'ui seeking only to serve, but the stench is unbearable to me. I am sure they realise this, although they feign ignorance. Yesterday a particularly foul smelling beast, named Omutu, spent the whole light-time following me around giving off a range of odours that amused the other Kroot but left me nauseous. I am sure he found it funny. I suppose I should be glad to discover that there is such a thing as Kroot humour.

Standing about 30% taller than us, the Kroot are lean and wiry. They have muscles like metal cables, able to pull taunt in an instant, giving them a jerky, deceptively fast gait. They can jump large distances when they need to and can manoeuvre through the branches of trees with practised ease. They seem to ignore shifts in climate and atmosphere. They have a rapport with other wildlife that is probably based on the fact that the Kroot are only interested in such life forms as food when they are dead. Although their own language is a mixture of clicks, squawks and hoots, the Kroot are superb mimics and are able to link sounds to a particular piece of body language very quickly. Last rotaa I spent a few decs teaching a Kroot youngling to speak Tau. He could make himself understood by dark-time and is now one of our escorts.

Whilst we cannot be certain, it is our current belief that the Kroot still have the capacity for further selective mutation. There seems to be several different approaches to achieving this among the Kroot. All Shapers seem to belong to one of a number of kindreds, each seeking a different path. This is the nearest thing to a nation we have found amongst the Kroot. We have evidence that each kindred has a fractionally different genetic code to the others. We immediately saw that, despite their apparent primitivism, the Kroot enjoyed a caste system related to our own. This reassured us considerably and, over our time, we have come to care for our hosts as the unsophisticated creatures they are. With our guidance they will prosper.

I have spoken with Shas'la Tau'n Droakan who most often guards us on our travels. He tells me that the Kroot are fearsome warriors and that now they are being supplied with charged rounds for their rifles, they will be a valuable addition to the Empire's forces. We have both remarked on how Pech has the vestigial traces of industry and manufacture, yet the Kroot lifestyle is wholly primitive. We have no idea how they can on the one hand operate their huge warspheres but on the other live in tree hives bound together with regurgitated dead wood. We have detected unusual energy emissions from some hills nearby and will investigate shortly.

The Shas'la has remarked to me that he has noticed a far greater variety of Kroot kindred on Pech than he has seen serving with our armies. This is odd as many of the Kroot on Pech are clearly warriors and liable under the terms of the annexation to military service. Last kai'rotaa I saw a warsphere disembarking its warriors among which there were many injured Kroot. I checked with Shas'ar'tol command and was told there had been no sanctioned combat involving Kroot recently. It is therefore my conclusion that many Kroot still pursue their old lifestyle as mercenaries outside the control of the Tau Empire. We were aware that not all Kroot were in agreement with annexation, so we assumed that the dissidents had left Pech to pursue a nomadic lifestyle. Their activities do not disturb us but their periodic return to Pech is at worse a destabilising influence and at best a brake on the progress we have planned for this species.

As I mentioned, there are many species on Pech which have emerged from the Kroot. We have identified three closely related species already.

The oldest stable form we have been able to find is a reclusive winged species about half the height of a normal Kroot. This variety of Kroothawk lives in remote nests at the top of the tallest jagga trees and is independent of the Kroot proper. The Kroot we questioned tell us that the Kroothawks are sacred to them and have always been the way they are. We have yet to secure a specimen for examination and have decided that it would be indiscreet to simply shoot one.

The Kroot hounds are undeniably descended from the same root as the Kroot themselves. We surmise that they are the remains of a previous kindred's selective mutations. Perhaps they sought to emulate a successful pack hunter but, whatever their intention, they became entirely locked into this one form. Evolution for them now is no different to that of Erijabirds in the orchards of the Aun'bork'an'retha. Their form is particularly vile though; while I have learned to regard the Kroot with some affection, I despise the Kroot hounds. They are slavering brutes which will kill even when they are well-fed. I once found myself alone in a glade when a Kroot hound happened by. It just stared at me, alternately sniffing and growling, the more nervous I got the more it growled. I am sure it would have attacked me but Mataba, the Shaper in charge of our escort, appeared out of the trees and, without any apparent communication, the Kroot hound slunk off.

The Krootox are different again. They wander the forest floor in large clans feeding off the moulds that cover the lower trunks of the jagga trees. They are huge creatures and are as strong as any warrior in a Crisis suit. They are short-tempered but essentially harmless. Just as the Kroot hounds are trapped in their feral form, the Krootox are trapped as grazing beasts. I suspect that they have a measure more intelligence, though, and have been impressed by their loyalty to the Kroot. When a Krootox is domesticated, it becomes attached to its masters to the extent that it will die to protect them. Droaken joked that they were as faithful to the Kroot as we are to the Ethereal ones. I chided him that there was more to our devotion than simple reaction to exuded chemical odours. The very thought! The Krootox are used as beasts of burden and are the most reliable of animals. When angered they are said to be terrifying, but I have yet to see them so. I have noted that the Kroot are careful not to mistreat them though.

There are many other species on Pech closely related to the Kroot. Mataba has warned me that some are outcast among the Kroot and are killed if found. I shudder to think the horror that Mataba considers worthy of a warning. The Shaper is a formidable creature and has served well.

So, sister, if the thinkers back home try to tell you that the Kroot are just primitives who don't deserve to share our destiny, you tell them they are wrong. It is wonderful that, because of the Empire, we can study such fascinating creatures and enlist their support in our great purpose. The next message boat will not be here for at least two kai'rotaa but I will write again then.

THE TAU ART OF WAR

ORIGINS

The Fire caste are the specialist warrior caste of the Tau – they have always been sturdier and more aggressive than the other castes and were successful plains hunters in their early history. Tau battle tactics still derive from the discipline of the hunt and are based on effective coordination of the hunters and correct selection of the position from which to make the kill and the weapon with which it is to be made.

ORGANISATION

Tau are organised in teams of warriors originating from the same sept, often bound by a Ta'lissera. These teams are grouped into Hunter Cadres under the leadership of a Commander and/or an Ethereal with the balance of teams selected for the particular hunt to be undertaken.

TAU TACTICAL PHILOSOPHY

The two most common forms of Hunter Cadre are the Mont'ka and Kauyon. Each method is taught by the great Fire caste academies on each Fire caste world and have their own adherents amongst the Shas'o and Shas'el masters. They are both based on hunting techniques. Broadly speaking, there are two approaches to hunting: the first involves bringing the prey to the hunter, the second involves the hunter running the prey to ground; the former is Kauyon, the latter Mont'ka.

Hunter Cadres average slightly more than fifty Tau and, in practice, a typical Tau army for Warhammer 40,000 represents a single Hunter Cadre.

MONT'KA – THE KILLING BLOW

Roughly translated, Mont'ka is the Killing Blow. It is the art of identifying a target of opportunity and attacking it swiftly with a Hunter Cadre, often deployed from a Manta Missile Destroyer. A Cadre pursuing the Mont'ka may stand in readiness for several days awaiting the command to strike. During this time they will plan the exact movements they will perform when the call comes. Often the decision to strike will come from a Shas'el or Shas'o with a good view of the enemy or the input of a well-sited Pathfinder team. It is firmly believed that the bond of trust between the Cadre which conducts the Mont'ka and the Commander who orders it brings honour to both. The attack will be immediately called off if the prey remains resilient or evasive.

KAUYON – THE PATIENT HUNTER

In the Tau language the words for hunter and patience are derived from the same root. This technique is the oldest of the Tau techniques and has the most variations. Essentially the technique relies on the interaction of the hunter and the lure. In recent times auxiliary troops such as Kroot are used as the lure, although some septs still regard the role as one that honours both hunter and prey and allow only bonded Fire warrior teams to undertake it.

The lure's role is to expose itself to the prey and draw it into a position where it can be killed by the hunter. The more subtle Commanders have been known to use the absence of troops as a lure. Once the prey is in position, the lure is free to escape or help the hunter as the situation dictates. Hunters are frequently equipped with Crisis, Stealth or Broadside armour with weapons carefully selected for the particular prey.

SIEGE

The Tau do not hold positions by choice. Defensively, the Earth caste construct bunkers and fortifications to provide shelter from long-range or aerial bombardment. Sometimes they construct a hidden bunker or Run'al to allow close observation of the enemy. Neither are intended for static defence.

The Fire caste are entirely committed to mobile warfare in which targets are identified, tracked and killed in an efficient and cautious manner. The Tau regard close combat as primitive and always plan their attacks around the application of firepower.

Tau cities are not fortified except under the direst circumstances and, wherever possible, they attempt to either draw enemy attacks away from them or slow the enemy advance while an evacuation is performed. Once a city is evacuated, the Tau will defend it just as they would a region of rocky ravines, and many variants of Kauyon are solely concerned with exploiting the peculiar layout of a city.

On the rare occasions when the Tau are absolutely compelled to defend a vital resource, they still apply their traditional techniques. In this case, the Mont'ka is applied as lightning fast forays out of the defences, each aimed at killing the enemy that pose the greatest threat. The Kauyon is represented by a feigned retreat from the perimeter to draw the attacker into a well-prepared kill zone.

On the offensive, Tau prefer not to attack cities by storm. Instead, they watch the main approaches and use the city as a lure to draw relief forces into ambushes. The Tau are good night fighters and when darkness falls they move into range of the defences and systematically destroy them.

When they absolutely must storm defences, the attack will be led by auxiliary troops such as the Kroot in a variation of Kauyon. The assault troops are not used as pawns – the Tau way of war does not recognise the concept of expendable troops. Instead their safety is entrusted to the troops providing the covering fire who must identify and kill enemy firebases before the assault force suffers serious harm. The Kroot are frequently used as stormers because their natural fieldcraft skills allow them to make the best use of natural cover as they advance. There is a Mont'ka variant where precisely planned strikes are launched (often by Crisis teams) against a careful selection of targets which, when destroyed, compromise the entire defensive position. This technique is the hallmark of a master strategist and will rarely be sanctioned otherwise.

BATTLE

As the Tau empire expands, the need to fight large scale engagements has caused the purist Fire caste approach to be questioned and, at the suggestion of the Ethereal caste, large numbers of auxiliaries have been incorporated into the Tau military, the most common being the mercenary Kroot. The auxiliaries are used to maintain a battle line around which the highly mobile Tau Hunter Cadres operate. This change has allowed the Tau to fight wars on a large scale where previously they would have been limited to raids.

Tau battle plans are very complex as each Hunter Cadre is assigned specific targets, locations and times. Teams are briefed at length beforehand and simulations are widely employed. The Tau may start a battle with elaborate flowing attacks, each launched with perfect planning, but sooner or later their prepared scenarios cease to apply and they lose momentum. When this occurs they will disengage and plan anew.

It is important to note that the Tau regard territorial gain as militarily irrelevant compared to the destruction of enemy forces. Ground is for position from which to make the kill; once the kill is made the ground is for the taking. A Tau army will gladly retreat from a strong enemy attack to preserve Tau lives while it awaits its opportunity to strike back decisively.

Tau attribute no dishonour to prudent retreat and see last stands as a lack of imagination or the last refuge of an incompetent commander. Unlike the Imperium of Man, the Tau empire cannot draw on limitless manpower, so the strategy of attrition is unknown to them.

The Fire caste is capable of battle rage and there have been occasions where the death of an especially beloved Ethereal has enraged an army beyond endurance. This does not result in them rushing into hand-to-hand combat. Instead they advance steadily while pouring an unceasing volume of fire into the enemy. Such an attack will only be halted by the expenditure of all ammunition.

GRAND TACTICAL EQUIPMENT

MANTA MISSILE DESTROYERS

The Manta Missile Destroyer is the nearest Tau equivalent of Human Titans or Ork Gargants. It is a dropship, several times larger than a Thunderhawk gunship, which is capable of operating as either a skimmer or a flyer on the battlefield. In space it is a match for whole squadrons of Imperial fighters and is on the borderline between being an attack craft and a full starship. It is equipped with an ether drive, but is not nearly as fast as a true starship over interstellar distances. Each Manta carries a full Hunter Cadre of between fifty and one hundred Tau. All the troops carried will either be mounted in gravitic vehicles or equipped with jet packs, and can all deploy from the Manta Missile Destroyer at altitude.

The Manta Missile Destroyer is well shielded and is armed with heavy railguns. The guns fire a heavy shell that uses fins for additional lift to give it remarkable range in atmosphere. Each shell is fitted with a Tau drone processor, which is programmed to direct the shell to its target. The drone is equipped with a manoeuvring thruster for this purpose. As the Manta nears its target, batteries of close-ranged ion cannons take over. It serves as a drop ship and heavy fire support for the Tau forces. Its distinctive silhouette is rightly feared by the Tau empire's enemies.

BARRACUDA SUPERIORITY FIGHTERS

The Barracuda is the most common Tau atmospheric flyer, although different Air caste septs tend to operate slightly different versions. The Barracuda is faster than the Imperial Marauder bomber, but slightly slower than the Thunderbolt fighter. Its electronic systems are very advanced, though, and it tends to achieve target locks quicker than the Thunderbolt. Barracudas carry wing-mounted, drone-controlled burst cannon and a pilot-aimed ion cannon. In case of damage, the pilot's cockpit is ejected intact and has limited gravitic mobility to return the pilot to safety. All pilots are of the Air caste and have superior three-dimensional situational awareness to Human pilots and marginally higher acceleration tolerance. This makes them naturally more gifted pilots, but the experience of the best Imperial pilots gives them a hard edge which the Air caste struggles to match.

TAU BATTLESUIT TECHNOLOGY

Tau technology is highly advanced and incorporates myriad integrated systems that enable the warriors in the Fire caste to wage war more efficiently. Much of the wargear comes in the form of battlesuit support systems that allow warriors to shoot extra weaponry or control combat drones. Other systems are hard-wired into the Tau themselves to provide advanced targeting mechanisms and improved sensors.

BATTLESUIT SYSTEMS

There are three types of Tau battlesuit. Their capabilities are summarised in the table below.

XV8 CRISIS	S	T	W	Save
	+2	+1	+1	3+

Jetpack, 3 weapon systems or support systems.

XV15 STEALTH	S	T	W	Save
	+1	–	–	3+

Jetpack, stealthsuit, burst cannon.

XV88 BROADSIDE	S	T	W	Save
	+2	+1	+1	2+

2 weapon systems, 1 support system.

In addition to the major features of each battlesuit type shown in the summary, all battlesuits have Recoil Absorption and Improved Sensors in common.

Improved Characteristics. Note that some Tau battlesuits improve their wearer's characteristics. This includes Toughness. When determining whether a model is killed outright by a weapon, the adjusted Toughness is used. So for example, if a plasma gun (Strength 7) wounded a Tau in Crisis armour, the Tau would only take 1 wound. This is different to the way that modified Toughness normally works in Warhammer 40,000 and reflects the fact that it is impossible for an attack to hit a battlesuit wearer without the suit at least partially absorbing the impact.

Recoil Absorption. All XV battlesuits are designed to compensate for the recoil of light weapons fire, so they do not count as moving when they fire rapid fire weapons. This ability does not extend to heavy weapons, however, and the user must be stationary to fire them. In this regard XV battlesuits are not as well stabilised as Space Marine Terminators but they do have a better range of weapons fits available.

Improved Sensors. Crisis, Stealth and Broadside battlesuits are equipped with a number of variable spectrum sensors and scanners. These sensors allow them to detect ambushes (Codex: Catachans p.20) or Lictors using secret deployment (Codex: Tyranids p.11). One member of a team may scan instead of shooting during the Shooting phase.

BATTLESUIT EQUIPMENT

The following equipment is fitted to specific battlesuit types and drones. They cannot be used with other battlesuits or by models not wearing battlesuits.

JETPACK

Tau jetpacks are extremely agile, combining anti-gravitic and jet technology.

A model with a jetpack can either:

• Move 6" in their Movement phase, ignoring intervening terrain as they fly over it like a model with a jump pack;

• Move up to 6" by walking or hovering just above the ground, as normal infantry;

They will also fall back and sweeping advance 3D6".

Troops equipped with jetpacks may Deep Strike when the mission permits. See the Warhammer 40,000 rulebook for details of Deep Strike.

An unbroken model with a jetpack that is not in close combat may always move 6" in the Assault phase whether they are within 6" of an enemy or not. This move may be in any direction. It does not have to be a charge towards the enemy, even if the jetpack wearer is within 6" of an enemy model. This move is always made like a model with a jump pack.

STEALTHSUIT

Stealthsuits incorporate a holographic disruption field that makes its wearer hard to spot. Enemy models attempting to fire at Stealth armour troopers count as if firing at night and must roll to check their spotting distance by rolling 2D6x3 (see the Warhammer 40,000 rulebook). If the Stealth armour troopers are not within spotting range, the unit misses its chance to fire while searching for a target and may not choose to fire at a different target. Stealth armour troopers count as being in cover if they are assaulted, but not if they charge. If firing at Stealthsuits while the Night Fighting scenario special rules are in effect, the rolled spotting distance is halved. Any drones controlled by a model in a Stealthsuit will also be shielded at no further cost in points.

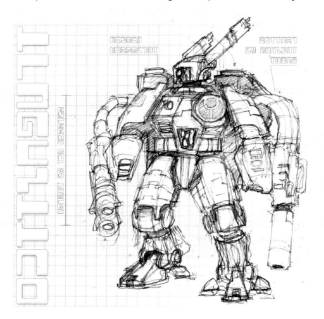

CRISIS BATTLESUIT WEAPONS

Each Crisis suit has three hard points, each of which MUST have a weapon or support system allocated to it. Each member of a Crisis team may carry a different combination of weapons if desired.

Crisis weapon systems are either: flamers, burst cannon, fusion blasters, rocket pods or plasma rifles.

It is possible to mount the same weapon system (not if it is a flamer though) on two hard points instead of one. The two weapons will then fire like a single twin-linked weapon. It is not possible to mount the same weapon on three hard points. Note that unless the multi-tracker support system is fitted, Tau battlesuits may only fire a single weapon type each turn.

BROADSIDE BATTLESUIT WEAPONS

Each Broadside battlesuit has three hard points. Broadside suits are capable of mounting far heavier weapons than Crisis suits, and a single Broadside hard point can be fitted with a twin-linked weapon. Each member of a Broadside team may carry a different combination of weapons if desired.

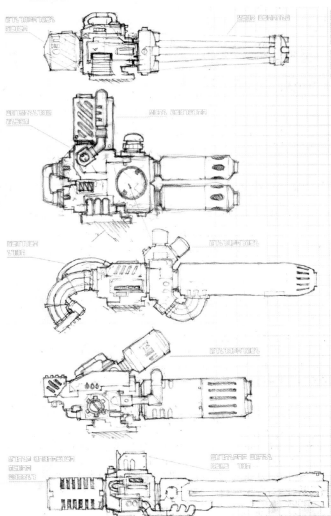

A pair of twin-linked railguns will always occupy one hard point. A second hard point will mount either a pair of twin-linked plasma rifles or a single smart missile system. The final hard point will always have a battlesuit support system assigned to it.

BATTLESUIT SUPPORT SYSTEMS

Support systems are not actually weapons as such but help to make the battlesuit wearer more effective in battle.

A model may not have more than one of the same support system.

Sensor – Multi-tracker
The multi-tracker enables the suit wearer to fire two Crisis or Broadside battlesuit weapon systems.

Sensor – Target lock
The target lock enables the model to target a separate enemy unit to that engaged by the rest of its own unit.

Shield generator
This confers a 4+ Invulnerable save.

Drone controller
A drone controller enables the suit wearer to command from 1 to 2 gun or shield drones.

BATTLESUIT WEAPONS

Weapon	Range	Str	AP	Type	Notes
Burst cannon	18"	5	5	Assault 3	
Flamer	Template	4	5	Assault 1	
Missile pod	36"	7	4	Assault 2	
Plasma rifle	24"	6	2	Rapid Fire	*1
Fusion blaster	12"	8	1	Assault 1	*2
Railgun (solid shot)	72"	10	1	Heavy 1	See below
Smart missile system	24"	5	5	Heavy 4	See below

Notes

*1 The Tau plasma rifle is lower powered than its Imperial equivalent but does not suffer from overheating.

*2 The Tau fusion blaster is similar to the Imperial meltagun in design and effect. Like the meltagun it rolls 2D6 for Armour Penetration if within 6" of the target.

Railguns. The Tau battlesuit railgun uses linear accelerator technology to project a solid projectile at hypervelocity. The vehicle mounted railgun can also fire submunitions but this option is not available to the battlesuit mounted version.

Smart Missile System. The smart missile system fires self-guiding missiles with the intelligence of a drone, which first search for then hunt down the target, passing around any blocking terrain.

The smart missile can engage any target in range regardless of whether there is a line of sight to it or not. The target can count the benefits of cover they are in or touching. If fighting at night, the range to the target is reduced as normal because the missile's sensors are less likely to identify and confirm the target.

WARGEAR OF THE TAU

HARD-WIRED SUPPORT SYSTEMS

In addition to their battlesuit systems, some Tau have support systems hard-wired in. These systems are cybernetic in nature and are either entirely contained within the battlesuit helmet or are implanted as warrior jewellery and cannot be removed without surgery.

The same model may not have more than one of each hard-wired support system and may not duplicate any battlesuit support system on the same model.

Multi-tracker

The multi-tracker enables the wearer to fire two weapon systems in the same turn. Normal Fire warriors would gain no benefit from this upgrade, as they cannot carry two weapons.

Target Lock

The target lock enables the suit wearer to target a separate enemy unit to that engaged by the rest of his own unit.

Blacksun Filter

The blacksun filter enables the user to see up to 4D6 x 3" when fighting at night. See the Warhammer 40,000 rulebook for details of night fighting.

Only models equipped with the blacksun filter gain any extra benefit. If for example a Broadside team leader has the filter and his team doesn't then only the team leader may fire at ranges above the normal 2D6 x 3" visibility distance at night.

Drone controller

A drone controller enables the suit wearer to select gun and shield drones. Each controller commands from 1 to 2 drones.

DRONES

Drones are independent artificial intelligences, programmed to protect the Tau. Unlike the Imperium, the Tau make extensive use of machine intelligences. The standard drone consists of an advanced processor, which individually is approximately as intelligent as a pterasquirrel.

The Drone unit is conventionally disc-shaped, well-armoured and used for both tedious and dangerous duties. Normally drones will require regular orders from a Tau but when several intelligences are networked together in a squadron they become capable of acting independently for a long period.

Drones, Objectives and Victory Points. Drones that are under the command of a drone controller are counted when assessing if the unit they are with should take a 25% Casualty test. They are similarly counted when determining if the unit is strong enough to claim an objective. If their unit suffers losses, drones are counted when determining if it is below 50% for victory point purposes.

If a unit consists entirely of drones (included as a separate Fast Attack choice or detached from a vehicle) it is treated as a normal unit except that it must be at least four models strong to hold an objective. This is the minimum number required to form a fully effective self-aware network.

Targeting Mixed Units. When shooting at Tau units containing drones, hits must be allocated before rolling to wound. All drones that can possibly be hit must have hits allocated to them before any are allocated to the rest of the unit. The Tau player allocates weapon hits to targets. For example, a team of three Tau Crisis battlesuits and two gun drones are hit by a lascannon, a plasma gun and three bolters. The Tau player takes the lascannon and plasma gun hits on the gun drones. The Crisis battlesuits are each hit by a bolter shot.

When assaulting Tau units containing drones, attacks must be allocated to drones where possible. Any model in base-to-base contact with a drone must attack it and any model not in base-to-base contact at all but within 2" of a drone must attack the drone.

If an attack form is specifically allowed to target a specific opponent – for example a Vindicare Assassin or a Farseer with Mind War – then drones are unable to intercede.

Controlled Drones. Drones must maintain coherency with the unit their controller is in. If he is an independent character then the drones and character form a unit but the character may still join another unit. If the character with the drone controller is killed then all his drones are removed at the end of the Shooting or Assault phase in which he died.

GUN DRONES

WS	BS	S	T	W	I	A	Ld	Sv
2	2	3	3	1	4	1	n/a	4+

Weapons: Twin-linked pulse carbine

SPECIAL RULES

Jetpack: Drones are equipped with Tau jetpacks.

Leadership: If in an independent squadron, gun drones have Leadership 7. If the number of drones in the squadron drops below 4 then their Leadership is reduced to 4.

SHIELD DRONE

WS	BS	S	T	W	I	A	Ld	Sv
2	2	3	3	1	4	1	n/a	4+*

Weapons: None

SPECIAL RULES

Jetpack: Drones are equipped with Tau jetpacks.

Invulnerable Save: The shield drone is equipped with several powerful energy shields and counter-measures and its 4+ save is Invulnerable.

OTHER WARGEAR.

Bonding Knife

This is a ceremonial knife, not intended for combat, carried by the leader of Fire caste warrior teams who have performed the Ta'lissera ritual and bonded as a group.

The bonded team may regroup even if below half strength. Battlesuit wearers need not actually carry the knife but may have a knife design painted onto their armour. However many Tau are in the team, they are all considered to be bonded for 10 points.

Photon Grenades

Identical to the grenades fired from the launcher on the pulse carbine, photon grenades are designed to assail the enemy with a sonic blast and an overpowering pulse of multi-spectrum light. They are hurled by hand to confuse and slow enemy closing to hand to hand combat. If a model has photon grenades then enemy assaulting them do not get any bonus attacks for charging. Photon grenades cannot be used with XV battlesuits.

EMP Grenades

EMP grenades briefly emit an electro-magnetic pulse which overloads circuitry, causing fires, meltdowns and other critical malfunctions. They are used when assaulting enemy vehicles. Each attacker may make one attack unadjusted for charging or additional close combat weapons. Roll to hit as normal. When determining damage, roll a D6. On a 4 or 5 they inflict a glancing hit, on a 6 they inflict a penetrating hit. They cannot be used against vehicles with WS that are not immobilised. EMP grenades cannot be used with XV battlesuits.

Honour Blade

This is a long, broad-bladed spear mounted on a lightweight metallic shaft. The honour blade is used to settle disputes between Ethereal caste members in stylised bloodless duels. It is used in elegant sweeping movements where the blade becomes virtually invisible. The honour blade must be used in two hands – the wielder cannot therefore count as carrying an additional weapon. It adds +2 to the wielder's Strength when rolling to wound.

Markerlight

Range: 36"   Strength: n/a   AP: n/a   Heavy 1

Models use markerlights as a weapon with the above profile instead of using their other weapons, rolling to hit normally. Each markerlight hit can be used to either launch a seeker missile or to mark a target for another vehicle or model. If marking a target then one other vehicle or model in the Tau force which has yet to fire can change its to hit roll against the same target to 2+ with a single weapon (regardless of its BS with that weapon) during the same Shooting phase. Re-rolls for twin-linked weapons still apply to the improved to hit roll.

TAU WEAPONRY

Pulse Rifle, Pulse Carbine or Burst Cannon

All three weapons are variants of the same technology. An induction field is used to propel a particle. The particle reacts by breaking down to create a plasma pulse as it leaves the barrel. The burst cannon is a multi-barrelled version of the carbine able to sustain high rates of fire but lacking the grenade launcher. The pulse carbine sacrifices range for portability and the chance to mount an underslung photon grenade launcher. Any unit suffering at least one wound from pulse carbine fire must test for pinning.

Hammerhead Railgun

The railgun is a linear accelerator which functions using standing wave acceleration along a number of cylindrical superconductive electrodes that surround the barrel. It can fire either a solid projectile or a sophisticated bundle of submunitions. The submunitions option is only available to the larger vehicle mounted railgun. The Ordnance template is used to determine how many models are hit by the submunition round, although the railgun is not an ordnance weapon.

Ion Cannon

Ion weaponry generates a stream of high-energy particles that are accelerated by an electromagnetic field. These will react explosively with the target as a result of direct transfer of energy at the atomic level.

Hammerhead Smart Missile System

The smart missile launcher fires a cluster of small missiles. Each missile is guided by a drone processor unit built into its warhead. Upon launch, the smart missile will search for targets before selecting and engaging one based on criteria previously detailed by its operator. It is therefore able to engage any enemy target in range even if the target cannot be seen by the firer.

Kroot Rifle

A basic slug-thrower relying on chemical propellant and the transfer of kinetic energy. The Tau have adapted the weapon to fire a charged pulse round supplied by them. The new ammunition gives the Kroot rifle far greater stopping power and penetration. The Kroot rifle is fitted with blades near the muzzle and stock. These are a throwback to early traditional Kroot fighting staves.

The incredible hand speed that a Kroot possesses due to its unique musculature makes these blades effective assault weapons and Kroot with Kroot rifles accordingly count as having an additional close combat weapon.

Weapon	Range	Str	AP	Type	Notes
Pulse Rifle	30"	5	5	Rapid Fire	
Pulse Carbine	18"	5	5	Assault 1	Pinning test
Railgun (solid shot)	72"	10	1	Heavy 1	
Ion Cannon	60"	7	3	Heavy 3	
Railgun (submunition)	72"	6	4	Heavy 1	Ordnance blast
Smart Missile System	24"	5	5	Heavy 4	No line of sight needed
Kroot Rifle	24"	4	6	Rapid Fire	See above
Kroot Gun	48"	7	4	Rapid Fire	

TAU VEHICLE UPGRADES

Sensor Spines

Sensor spines are arrayed over a vehicle to allow it to detect a range of hazards. These sensors allow them to detect ambushes (Codex: Catachans, p.20) and secret deployment (Lictors, Codex: Tyranids, p.11). They may shoot and scan in the same Shooting phase. Additionally a vehicle fitted with sensor spines will only trigger a mine when passing over a minefield on a roll of 6.

Multi-tracker

The vehicle-mounted multi-tracker is combined with advanced stabilisers enabling a vehicle to fire as if it were a fast vehicle. Thus a vehicle can fire one weapon if moving up to 12", or all of its weapons if moving up to 6".

Targeting Array

Targeting arrays assist the vehicle gunner's aim by adjusting for the target's range and speed. Add 1 to the vehicle's BS.

Blacksun Filter

This is simply a vehicle-mounted version of the hard-wired blacksun filter. The vehicle rolls 4D6 x 3 for visibility distance when subject to the Night Fighting mission special rules and traces line of sight normally.

Gun Drones

A vehicle may be equipped with two gun drones. The drones will move with the vehicle, safely contained in specially designed recesses. During any Tau Movement phase, the drones may disengage in the same way as infantry dismount from a transport and form an independent unit. From then on, the drones function as a Drone squadron. The drones may not rejoin the vehicle during a game.

While attached, the gun drones may fire as part of the vehicle, using their own BS, in addition to any other weapons that would normally be permitted to fire, and are treated as passengers if the vehicle is damaged.

Flechette Discharger

Powerful clusters of reactive charges are attached to the prows of many Tau vehicles. If the vehicle moves into close proximity of an enemy they fire off vicious clouds of high velocity flechettes. If an enemy model elects to make a death or glory attempt during a tank shock attack by a vehicle equipped with flechette dischargers, it must first pass an Armour saving throw or suffer one wound.

Decoy Launchers

Decoy launchers are mounted near the engines of Tau skimmers and fire clouds of reflective strips and tiny emitter drones to protect the vulnerable thruster arrays. Whenever a glancing hit result of 4 (Immobilised) is rolled against the vehicle, the decoy launchers will force the damage dice to be re-rolled. The decoy launcher can only force one re-roll so the second result stands, even it is immobilised again.

Disruption Pod

A disruption pod throws out distorting images in both visual and magnetic spectra, making it hard to target at long range. Weapons firing at the vehicle have their range reduced by 6", down to a minimum of 24" or the weapon range if less.

Target Lock

The target lock identifies potential targets and plots fire plans to counter them, granting the vehicle gunner far more choice about the targets to be engaged. Each weapon on the vehicle may fire at a separate enemy unit if desired, subject to the normal line of sight rules.

Seeker Missiles

Seeker missile arrays are provided to allow Tau infantry to immediately obtain fire support. Any model equipped with a markerlight may request a single missile to be launched if they score a hit on the desired target with their markerlight.

Up to four missiles can be fitted to a single vehicle and launched in a single turn if desired, although each needs to be guided by a separate markerlight. Each missile is a one-shot weapon.

The missiles do not need a line of sight from the vehicle they are mounted on to the target, and they hit on a 2+. The missile is assumed to move in a straight line between the model carrying the missile and the target itself for the purposes of deciding whether the shot strikes the front, side or rear. The target may count the benefits of cover they are in or immediately behind.

The vehicle carrying the seeker missiles has no control over them and cannot launch them itself. The mechanism is remote and responds only to markerlight users.

Range: unlimited   Strength: 8   AP: 3   Heavy 1

TAU ARMOURY

An Ethereal caste member, any Fire caste member of Shas'vre rank or higher, or a Shas'Ui team leader may select items from the following list. No model may have more than 50 points of equipment from the Armoury.

HARD-WIRED SUPPORT SYSTEMS

A Commander may have up to three hard-wired systems, otherwise each model may have only one hard-wired system.

Hard-wired multi-tracker . . . . 10 pts	Hard-wired blacksun filter . . . . 3 pts
Hard-wired target lock . . . . 7 pts	Hard-wired drone controller . . . . 2 pts

DRONES

Gun drone (Must have drone controller) . . . . . . 10 pts	Shield drone (Must have drone controller) . . . . . . 15 pts

TAU VEHICLE UPGRADES

Tau vehicles can have additional systems as outlined in their army list entry. Any vehicle upgrades must be represented on the model. Apart from the seeker missile, no more than one of each upgrade may be mounted on the same model.

Sensor spines . . . . 5 pts	Pair of gun drones . . . . 20 pts
Targeting array . . . . 5 pts	Flechette discharger . . . . 5 pts
Multi-tracker . . . . 10 pts	Disruption pod . . . . 5 pts
Blacksun filter . . . . 5 pts	Decoy launchers . . . . 5 pts
Target lock . . . . 5 pts	Seeker missile . . . . . . (*up to 4 per vehicle*) 10 pts each

TAU ARMY LIST

This section of the book is given over to the Tau army list, a listing of the different troops and vehicles a Tau commander can use in battle, or in your case games of Warhammer 40,000. The army list allows you to fight battles using the scenarios included in the Warhammer 40,000 rulebook, but it also provides you with the basic information you'll require to field a Tau army in scenarios you've devised yourself, or as part of a campaign series of games, or what ever else may take your fancy.

The army list is split into five sections. All of the teams, squads, vehicles and characters in an army list are placed in one of the five sections depending upon their role on the battlefield. Also every model included in the army list is given a points value, which varies depending upon how effective that model is on the battlefield.

Before you can choose an army for a game you will need to agree with your opponent upon a scenario and upon the total number of points each of you will spend on your army. Having done this you can proceed to pick an army as described below.

USING A FORCE ORGANISATION CHART

The army lists are used in conjunction with the Force Organisation chart from a scenario. Each Force Organisation chart is split into five categories that correspond to the sections in the army list, and each catagory has one or more boxes. Each box indicates that you may make one choice from that section of the army list, while a dark toned box means that you must make a choice from that section.

USING THE ARMY LISTS

To make a choice, look in the relevant section in the army list and decide what unit you wish to have in your army, how many models there will be in the unit and which upgrades that you want (if any). Remember that you cannot field models that are equipped with weapons and wargear not shown on the model. Once this is done subtract the points value of the unit from your total points, and then go back and make another choice. Continue doing this until you have spent all your points. Now you are ready to continue the dynamic expansion of the Tau empire.

ARMY LIST ENTRIES

Each army list entry consists of the following:

Unit Name: The type of unit, which may also show a limitation on the maximum number of choices you can make of that unit type (0-1, for example).

Profile: These are the characteristics of that unit type, including its points cost. Where the unit has different warriors, there may be more than one profile.

Number/Team/Squad etc: This shows the number of models in the unit, or the number of models you may take for one choice from the Force Organisation chart. Often this is a variable amount, in which case it shows the minimum and maximum unit size.

Equipment: These are the unit's standard weapons and equipment.

Options: This lists the different weapon and equipment options for the unit and any additional points cost for taking these options.

Character: Some entries may include an option to upgrade one team member to a character. If a team is allowed to have models with upgrades then these must be given to ordinary team members, not the character.

Transport: If a unit is allowed to be mounted in a transport, this is mentioned here.

Special Rules: This is where you'll find any special rules that apply to the unit.

SPECIAL TAU NOTES

Strategy Rating
The Tau have a strategy rating of 1.

Sentries
When required to deploy sentries, the Tau player may use either 6 gun drones or 8 Kroot.

Experience
When playing Tau in a campaign in which experience is being counted then experience is accumulated in the same way as normal. Drone squadrons never gain experience. The experience deduction for being reduced below 50% only takes effect if the unit loses more than 50% of non-drone models.

A Tau unit which captures the survival pod at the end of the Hostage Situation mission (page 62) receives +300 experience if it is Tau, or +100 experience if it is Kroot.

Tau XV battlesuit units roll on the Bike/Cavalry Battle Honours table, Hammerheads and Devilfish on the Vehicle Battle Honours table, and all other units on the Infantry Battle Honours table. Any unit which rolls the Steadfast Infantry Battle Honour must re-roll it if they are bonded. If they are not bonded then they may be upgraded to bonded at no extra cost.

Tau vehicles have a Leadership of 7.

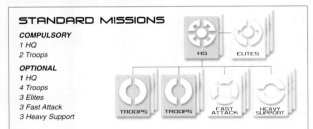

STANDARD MISSIONS

COMPULSORY
1 HQ
2 Troops

OPTIONAL
1 HQ
4 Troops
3 Elites
3 Fast Attack
3 Heavy Support

The Standard Missions Force Organisation chart is a good example of how to choose an army. To begin with you will need at least one HQ unit and two Troops units (dark shaded boxes indicate units that <u>must</u> be taken for the mission). This leaves the following for you to choose from to make up your army's total points value: up to 1 HQ unit, 0-3 additional Elite units, 0-4 additional Troop units, 0-3 additional Fast Attack units or 0-3 additional Heavy Support units.

HQ

COMMANDER(TAU: SHAS'EL OR SHAS'O)

	Points	WS	BS	S	T	W	I	A	Ld	Sv
Shas'o	75	4	5	5	4	4	3	4	10	3+
Shas'el	50	3	4	5	4	3	3	3	9	3+

Commander is a position of great honour for Tau of the Fire caste. It is attained only after years progressing through the ranks of Fire warriors to fight first in the battlesuit teams and then as part of another Commander's bodyguard. Proof of accomplishment in not only the tactical but also the strategic arts of war may then earn the Commander's approval and elevation from Shas'vre. Tau Commanders are formidable warriors, frequently sporting scars, bionics and disfigurements earned in their career. According to their renown they may be called upon to command anything from a Cadre to a Battle. The number and size of previous commands is reflected in the rings confining their long scalp locks. A Shas'el can only progress to the rank of Shas'o after repeated success in the field.

Equipment: Commanders are always equipped with an XV8 Crisis battlesuit. The above profile has been amended to include the suit's enhancements. In addition he may select additional equipment from the Tau Armoury.

SPECIAL RULES

Independent Character: Unless accompanied by a Bodyguard, the Commander is an Independent Character and follows the independent character special rules in the Warhammer 40,000 rulebook. If accompanied by drones, he may still join other units as an Independent Character .

Bodyguard: The Commander may be accompanied by a Bodyguard, see the separate entry below. The Commander and his Bodyguard count as a single HQ choice.

XV8 CRISIS BATTLESUIT HARD POINT OPTIONS

See 'Tau Battlesuit Technology'. Must fill all three hard points.

Flamer . . . .+6 pts
Burst cannon . . . .+10 pts, +15 pts if twin-linked*
Plasma rifle . . . .+16 pts, +24 pts if twin-linked*
Fusion blaster . . . .+12 pts, +18 pts if twin-linked*
Missile pod . . . .+14 pts, +21 pts if twin-linked*
Occupies two hard points if twin-linked

Multi-tracker . . . .+5 pts
Target lock . . . .+5 pts
Shield generator . . . .+20 pts
Drone controller plus from 1 to 2 gun drones . . . .+10 pts each drone
Drone controller plus from 1 to 2 shield drones . . . .+15 pts each drone

"Learn to shorten you reach!
If your foe can come close enough
to negate your striking power,
all stratagem is lost
and when all stratagem is lost,
the battle is lost."

ATTR O'SHOVAH 757.M41

0-1 ETHEREAL CASTE MEMBER [TAU: AUN]

	Points	WS	BS	S	T	W	I	A	Ld	Sv
Ethereal	50	4	3	3	3	2	3	3	10	-

Equipment: The Ethereal normally carries symbols of office that can be used as a pair of close combat weapons (+1 Attack). These may be exchanged for an honour blade for +10 points. He may select equipment from the Tau Armoury.

SPECIAL RULES

Independent Character: The Ethereal is an Independent Character and follows the independent character special rules in the Warhammer 40,000 rulebook. If accompanied by Drones, the Ethereal may still join friendly units.

Inspiring Presence: Tau units (not Kroot or Drones) may re-roll any Morale checks if there is a friendly Ethereal on the table. This includes passed Morale checks. The re-rolled result stands. Any Tau units joined by an Ethereal caste member become Fearless, and automatically pass all Morale checks and Pinning tests.

Price of Failure: Whilst the Tau are inspired by the presence of the Ethereals, they are conditioned to dread their death above all things. If a friendly Ethereal is killed then every unit of Tau on the tabletop (not Kroot or Drones) must take a Morale check at the start of their next turn if they are not in close combat or already falling back. Any that fail must Fall Back in their Movement phase but can attempt to regroup as normal afterwards.

Little is known of the Tau Ethereal caste, appearing as shrouded, enigmatic figures that eschew the advanced equipment favoured by the Tau Fire caste. Ethereals seem to combine the roles of priesthood and royalty within Tau society, and command unquestioning loyalty from all of the other castes. Ethereal caste members are occasionally seen on the battlefield, although whether leading or observing is unclear.

XV8 'CRISIS' BATTLESUIT BODYGUARD TEAM [TAU SHAS'VRE]

	Points	WS	BS	S	T	W	I	A	Ld	Sv
Shas'vre	40	3	3	5	4	2	3	2	8	3+

Team: A team consists of 1-2 Shas'vre. There can only be 0-1 team per Commander.

Equipment: Shas'vre bodyguards are always equipped with an XV8 Crisis battlesuit. The above profile has been amended to include the suit's enhancements. They may also select additional equipment from the Tau Armoury.

SPECIAL RULES

Bonded: The team may be bonded by the Ta'lissera at a cost of +10 points for the whole team. They will not carry a bonding knife but will have a knife design painted onto their battlesuits.

XV8 CRISIS BATTLESUIT HARD POINT OPTIONS
See 'Tau Battlesuit Technology'. Must fill all three hard points.

Flamer	+6 pts
Burst cannon	+10 pts, +15 pts if twin-linked*
Plasma rifle	+16 pts, +24 pts if twin-linked*
Fusion blaster	+12 pts, +18 pts if twin-linked*
Missile pod	+14 pts, +21 pts if twin-linked*

Occupies two hard points if twin-linked

Multi-tracker	+5 pts
Target lock	+5 pts
Shield generator	+20 pts
Drone controller plus from 1 to 2 gun drones	+10 pts each drone
Drone controller plus from 1 to 2 shield drones	+15 pts each drone

A Bodyguard team of Fire Warriors in Crisis battlesuit armour may accompany a Shas'o or a Shas'el. The bodyguards will always be Shas'vre veterans, experienced and proven in battle. It is common for such Bodyguard teams to be predominantly made up of the Commander's kin or long-term friends, and it is a great honour to be chosen for such duty. The bodyguard embody the Tau philosophy of striving for the greater good at the expense of personal glory and these warriors are much respected by the rest of the army.

ELITE

XV8 'CRISIS' BATTLESUIT TEAM (TAU: SHAS'UI)

	Points	WS	BS	S	T	W	I	A	Ld	Sv
Shas'ui	30	2	3	5	4	2	2	2	8	3+
Shas'vre	+10	3	3	5	4	2	3	2	8	3+

Those Fire warriors who prove themselves in battle earn the right to wear a battlesuit and bear the name of Shas'ui. They are experienced fighters who have fought the deadliest foes and triumphed. Their loyalty and skill is beyond question and the best and bravest of them may be honoured by being elevated to become a bodyguard to their Shas'o or Shas'el. Teams of Crisis battlesuit warriors will have fought together for many years and, in many cases, will have performed the Ta'lissera ritual where the warriors swear oaths of communion and loyalty to one another, placing the welfare of the team ahead of their own personal desires.

Team: A team consists of 1-3 Shas'ui.

Equipment: Crisis teams are equipped with an XV8 Crisis battlesuit. The above profile has been amended to include the suit's enhancements.

Character: One Shas'ui per team may be designated as a team leader at +5 points. They may then select items from the Tau Armoury. A Shas'ui team leader can be upgraded to Shas'vre for an additional +5 points.

SPECIAL RULES
Bonded: The team may be bonded by the Ta'lissera at a cost of +10 points for the whole team. They will not carry a bonding knife but will have a knife design painted onto their battlesuits.

XV8 CRISIS BATTLESUIT HARD POINT OPTIONS
See 'Tau Battlesuit Technology'. Must fill all three hard points.

Flamer	+6 pts
Burst cannon	+10 pts, +15 pts if twin-linked*
Plasma rifle	+16 pts, +24 pts if twin-linked*
Fusion blaster	+12 pts, +18 pts if twin-linked*
Missile pod	+14 pts, +21 pts if twin-linked*

*Occupies two hard points if twin-linked

Multi-tracker	+5 pts
Target lock	+5 pts
Shield generator	+20 pts
Drone controller plus from 1 to 2 gun drones	+10 pts each drone
Drone controller plus from 1 to 2 shield drones	+15 pts each drone

> "There are two kinds of conduct the Ethereals will not countenance. The first is a failure to reflect upon what is for the Greater Good of the Tau race. The second is the deliberate refusal to follow the path of the Greater Good when it is clear what it must be."
>
> POR'UI DAL'YTH UKOS, WATER CASTE ENVOY

XV15 STEALTH TEAM (TAU: SHAS'UI)

	Points	WS	BS	S	T	W	I	A	Ld	Sv
Shas'ui	30	2	3	4	3	1	2	2	8	3+
Shas'vre	+10	3	3	4	3	1	3	2	8	3+

Team: A team consists of 3-6 Shas'ui.

Equipment: Stealth teams are equipped with the XV15 Stealth battlesuit. The above profile is amended to include the suit's enhancements.

Character: One Shas'ui per team may be designated as a team leader at +5 points. They may then select items from the Tau Armoury. A Shas'ui team leader can be updated to Shas'vre at +5 points. The team leader may also buy a markerlight at an additional +10 points.

SPECIAL RULES

Stealth armour: Enemy models attempting to fire at Stealth armour troopers must roll to check their spotting distance by rolling 2D6x3 as if firing at night. If the Stealth armour troopers are not within spotting range, the unit may not choose to fire at a different target. Stealth armour troopers count as being in cover if they are assaulted. If firing at Stealthsuits while the Night Fighting scenario special rules are in effect, the rolled spotting distance is halved. Any drones controlled by a model in a Stealthsuit will also be shielded at no further cost in points.

Infiltrate: Stealth armour teams can use their suits to move into forward positions ahead of the main army unseen. To represent this they can set up using the Infiltrators scenario special rule if the mission allows it. Any drones attached to the unit may accompany them. If the mission does not allow troops to use the Infiltrate rule then the Stealth armour troops must set up with the rest of the army.

Bonded: The team may be bonded by the Ta'lissera at a cost of +10 points for the whole team. They will not carry a bonding knife but will have a knife design painted onto their battlesuits.

Stealth teams are the 'lone wolves' of the Tau army, operating independently of the other formations, intent on ambushing isolated enemy troops and intervening in support of friendly units. They are not factored directly into Tau battle plans and so enjoy a great deal of freedom of action within very broad parameters. The leaders of Stealth teams are often regarded as being slightly eccentric and delight in employing new and unpredictable tactics. Many a foe of the Tau empire has found himself attacked from an unexpected quarter by Stealth teams positioned ahead of the main army.

"I have received your messages, acquainting me that these worlds belong to your Emperor, your master. In return I am to inform you that the said worlds belong to his Ethereal Majesty, Aun'O Bork'an Vral, my master, by right of settlement. Should you wish to gain similar rights you must submit yourselves to his wisdom as members of the Tau empire."

POR'EL TAU'N UKOS, WATER CASTE NEGOTIATOR

"It is well that they are known as the Water caste.
One might as well try to nail the sea to the wall as pin them down with a straight answer.
They flow around your words until they wear you down, like the trickle of water that over time will split the rock."

ROGUE TRADER GUARNERIUS

TROOPS

1+ FIRE WARRIOR TEAM [TAU: SHAS'LA]

	Points	WS	BS	S	T	W	I	A	Ld	Sv
Shas'la	10	2	3	3	3	1	2	1	7	4+
Shas'ui	+10	2	3	3	3	1	2	2	8	4+

Fire warrior teams are ever-present in Tau armies and are formed from members of the same sept. They are cautious but efficient, and their pulse rifle armament gives them excellent firepower. Often mounted in a Devilfish troop carrier, they are able to rapidly deploy and lay down a withering fusillade upon their foes.

Team: The team consists of 6-12 Fire warriors.

Equipment: Pulse rifle.

Options: Up to half of the Fire warriors in the team (round fractions down) may exchange their pulse rifle for a pulse carbine at no extra points cost. The team may carry photon grenades at an additional cost of +1 point per model and EMP grenades at an additional cost of +3 points per model.

Character: One Fire warrior Shas'la may be upgraded to a Shas'ui team leader at an additional cost of +10 pts. The Shas'ui may be given extra equipment from the Tau Armoury. The Shas'ui may also buy a markerlight at an additional +10 points.

SPECIAL RULES
Bonded: A team may be bonded by the Ta'lissera at an additional cost of +10 points for the whole team.

Transport: If it numbers twelve models or less (including Drones), the team may be mounted in a Devilfish troop carrier.

TRANSPORT: DEVILFISH TROOP CARRIER

	Points	Armour: Front	Side	Rear	BS
Devilfish	80	12	11	10	3

The Devilfish troop carrier is the workhorse of the Tau ground forces and is able to carry twelve warriors. Armed with a fearsome Burst cannon, it can rapidly transport its passengers to their destination then act as mobile fire support once they have disembarked. The Devilfish also carries a pair of gun drones to provide even more firepower.

Type: Tank, Skimmer. **Crew:** Tau Fire caste.

Weapons: Burst cannon.

Systems: The Devilfish has the gun drone vehicle upgrade at no additional cost.

Options: The Devilfish may be equipped with any of the vehicle upgrades specified in the Tau Armoury. It may not select the gun drone upgrade again.

Transport: The Devilfish can carry up to twelve models. It may not carry any troops in XV battlesuits.

Access Points: There are access hatches at the rear and on each side of the hull. Models embarking or disembarking must be within 2" of one of them.

Fire Points: There are no fire points; the Devilfish is a pressurised environment. This means that passengers may not fire while aboard the vehicle.

> *"A thousand fibres connect each of us with our fellow Tau and along those fibres our deeds run as causes which come back to us as effects. Everything we do must be in furtherance of the Greater Good lest we return to the Mont'au, the Terror."*
>
> SHAS'O VIOR'LA KAIS, FIRE WARRIOR COMMANDER

KROOT CARNIVORE SQUAD

	Points	WS	BS	S	T	W	I	A	Ld	Sv
Kroot	7	4	3	4	3	1	3	1	7/8	-
Shaper	+21	4	3	4	3	3	3	3	7/8	6+

Squad: The squad numbers from 10-20 Kroot.

Equipment: Kroot rifle.

Options: If a Shaper is included in a Carnivore squad, the Kroot may acquire a 6+ armour save at a cost of +1 point per model. Some Shapers carry weaponry gifted from the Tau. For an additional +5 points, the Shaper's Kroot rifle can be replaced with either a pulse rifle or a pulse carbine.

Character: One Kroot may be upgraded to a Shaper at an additional cost of + 21 points.

SPECIAL RULES
Mercenaries: Kroot are mercenaries; they don't fight for idealism or noble causes, they fight for reward! To represent this, the Leadership characteristic of Kroot is not fixed, instead it is considered to be equal to their points value. Normally it is 7, but if they are upgraded with an improved Armour save it will increase to 8 (because they're 8 points then). Note that the presence of a Kroot Shaper, Kroot Hounds or Krootox doesn't directly affect the Leadership of the squad which is always based on the points cost of the standard Kroot carnivores.

Eaters of the Dead: Kroot are extremely voracious carnivores and will often let a defeated enemy escape while they feast on the flesh of the fallen. Kroot must pass a Leadership test in order to pursue a foe defeated in close combat or make a sweeping advance. If the test is failed the Kroot must consolidate. If a Kroot Shaper is in the squad then they MUST consolidate.

Fieldcraft: Kroot are naturally adept in arboreal environments and gain +1 to their cover save in woods or jungles. Kroot in woods or jungles do not have to roll a Difficult Terrain test; they can always move up to 6". If they do not move in the Movement phase they may see and shoot through 12" of woods or jungle terrain rather than the 6" that would normally be the case.

Infiltrate: If the squad does not contain a Krootox it may Infiltrate if the mission permits it. See the Warhammer 40,000 rulebook for the Infiltrators scenario special rules.

Kroot Hounds and Krootox: Carnivore Squads may have Kroot Hounds or Krootox attached to their unit – see the list entries for details. The combined unit counts as a single Troop choice from deployment onwards, although it may occupy several selections on the Force Organisation chart, and is also treated as such for Victory points purposes.

Kroot Carnivore squads are the most common auxiliaries serving alongside the Tau armies. The Kroot worlds have long been part of the empire, ever since a Tau expeditionary force helped liberate several Kroot enclaves from Ork domination. The Kroot warriors have a strict code of honour and, in return for the support of the Tau empire, supply large numbers of warriors as exclusive mercenaries. Their self-sufficiency and unparalleled fieldcraft are a major asset to the Tau and a useful contrast to their more technologically dependent masters. Kroot squads may also contain the lumbering Krootox and agile Kroot Hounds. Whilst the Tau find the Kroot's predilection for eating the flesh of their vanquished foes barbaric, it is hoped that prolonged exposure to the Tau's sensibilities and culture will eventually purge them of this distasteful habit. Despite this, the Kroot are afforded virtually the same level of respect as a Tau, since their skill at arms is much valued by the less physically able Tau. The Kroot are honoured for their martial prowess and are rewarded for their efforts, as befits loyal citizens of the Tau empire.

"It is as we join with others, in a way that only the Tau can, in shared engagement to the Greater Good, that we find ourselves able to fully realise our true potential. And that is the final source of our hopes and intentions."

AUN'EL T'AU TAM'YA, ETHEREAL CASTE

FAST ATTACK

GUN DRONE SQUADRON (TAU: KOR'VESA)

	Points	WS	BS	S	T	W	I	A	Ld	Sv
Gun Drone	12	2	2	3	3	1	4	1	7	4+

Squadron: The squadron numbers from 4-8 gun drones.

Equipment: Twin-linked pulse carbine.

Jetpacks: Drones are equipped with Tau jetpacks and can use these to Deep Strike as described in the jetpack wargear entry.

SPECIAL RULES

Independent: A Gun Drone squadron has its processors linked to enable it to have the capacity for independent action. They are programmed for self-preservation and take Leadership tests normally. If their numbers are reduced to less than 4 their Leadership drops to 4.

Acting in support of Fire warrior teams and armed with twin-linked pulse carbines, squadrons of gun drones can pin enemy troops in place while the main body of the Tau army takes further shots at the advancing enemy.

PATHFINDER TEAM (TAU: SHAS'LA)

	Points	WS	BS	S	T	W	I	A	Ld	Sv
Shas'la	12	2	3	3	3	1	2	1	7	4+
Shas'ui	+10	2	3	3	3	1	2	2	8	4+

Team: Consists of 4-8 Pathfinders.

Equipment: Pulse carbine with markerlight target designator.

Options: Pathfinders may carry photon grenades at an additional cost of +1 point per model and EMP grenades at an additional cost of +3 points per model.

Character: One Pathfinder Shas'la may be upgraded to a Shas'ui team leader at an additional cost of +10 points. The Shas'ui may be given extra equipment from the Tau Armoury.

SPECIAL RULES

Bonded: A team may be bonded by the Ta'lissera at an additional cost of +10 points for the whole team.

Forward Scouts: Pathfinders operate ahead of the main Tau lines identifying targets for Broadside and Crisis teams to eliminate. In scenarios where some troops start in reserve and others on table, Pathfinders always deploy on table. Pathfinders may make a normal move after deployment but before the first turn to get into a forward position. This move may include disembarking from the Devilfish.

Transport: Pathfinders **must** select a Devilfish troop carrier at an additional cost of +80 points.

Tau Pathfinders are the eyes and ears of the army's commander, and coordinate closely with other formations. An efficient Pathfinder team can help other Fire Warrior teams operate at peak efficiency and are highly respected as a consequence. They are the undisputed masters of battlefield positioning, with limitless patience and a proud determination to choose the most valuable targets for others to destroy. Imperial troops who fought in the Damocles Crusade described the signature of the barely visible markerlight beams as the Valkyrie's Mark, because those it chose were soon numbered among the dead.

KROOT HOUND PACK

	Points	WS	BS	S	T	W	I	A	Ld	Sv
Kroot Hound	6	4	0	4	3	1	4	2	*	*

Pack: A pack consists of 2-8 Kroot Hounds.

Equipment: Fangs.

SPECIAL RULES

Attached Unit: Kroot Hounds do not function as a separate unit on the tabletop. Although they occupy a Force Organisation chart Fast Attack choice, they must be attached to a Kroot Carnivore squad before the game.

They are deployed along with the Kroot Carnivore squad as if they were all a single Troops choice selection from the Force Organisation chart. There cannot be more models (counting Kroot Hounds and Krootox) added to a Carnivore squad than it initially consists of.

* Kroot Hounds, once attached, function as part of the Carnivore squad they are attached to. Their Leadership and Armour save will be the same as that of the Kroot unit they are attached to.

Release the Hounds: Whilst the Kroot themselves rarely pursue beaten enemy, the Kroot Hounds will pursue viciously for a while before returning to their unit. If enemy Fall Back from close combat with a Kroot unit, each Kroot Hound will inflict a single automatic Strength 4 hit on an enemy model.

Kroot Hounds are ferocious in battle and are notoriously bad-tempered beasts. Even in times of peace it is not unknown for a Kroot Hound to turn on its handler if he is careless enough to let his guard down. While the Tau value the strength and viciousness of the Kroot themselves, they find the Kroot Hounds repellent.

"They are fierce indeed these Kroot, and savage. I look upon them and tremble at their ferocity. I can only hope that when the enemy sees them they tremble as I do."

POR'VRE TAU CHO - WATER CASTE ENVOY TO SYL'KELL PRIOR TO THE AMBUSH OF THE 17TH BRIMLOCK DRAGOONS.

XV-88 BROADSIDE BATTLESUIT TEAM [TAU: SHAS'UI] ▭ ▢

	Points	WS	BS	S	T	W	I	A	Ld	Sv
Shas'ui	70	2	3	5	4	2	2	2	8	2+
Shas'vre	+10	3	3	5	4	2	3	2	8	2+

Team: Consists of 1-3 Broadside Shas'ui.

Equipment: Each member of the team is equipped with XV-88 Broadside armour. The above profile has been amended to include the suit's enhancements.

Character: One Shas'ui per team may be designated as a team leader at +5 points. They may then select items from the Tau Armoury. A Shas'ui team leader can be updated to Shas'vre at +5 points.

SPECIAL RULES
Bonded: The team may be bonded by the Ta'lissera at a cost of +10 points for the whole team. They will not carry a bonding knife but will have a knife design painted onto their battlesuits.

XV88 BROADSIDE BATTLESUIT HARD POINT OPTIONS
See 'Tau Battlesuit Technology'.

Twin-linked railgun and smart missile system.

May replace smart missile system with twin-linked plasma rifle at +10 pts.

Choose one support system from the following list:

Multi-tracker . . . .+5 pts
Target lock . . . .+5 pts
Shield generator . . . .+20 pts
Drone controller plus from 1 to 2 gun drones . . . .+10 pts each drone
Drone controller plus from 1 to 2 shield drones . . . .+15 pts each drone

Experienced veterans can wear Broadside Battlesuits and are the most heavily armed of all Tau ground troops. Broadside teams utilise a heavily modified version of the Crisis Battlesuit armour. The standard jetpack is removed, which frees up weight for the incorporation of some extremely heavy weapon systems. Broadside teams must be able to engage and destroy heavily armoured targets and, consequently, are equipped with the most devastating weapons in the Tau arsenal.

> "They got ded big shooty guns dat'll kill tons of boyz, but if yer can get near em den you've got a chance. Just gotta make sure you bring loads of boyz, coz you ain't gonna have a whole lot left when you get close enough ta crump em."
>
> WARLORD SKARMORK THE GREAT DESPOILER

> "Our tanks were useless. As soon as we broke cover, their battlesuits' heavy guns were locked on to us. I swear it was as though they had someone nearby aiming for them before they shot. And when they did shoot... Emperor's mercy! Their guns punched through our armour like it was paper. All I could see were trails of fire where the projectiles had ignited the air."
>
> GUARDSMAN CAULEY, 25TH GRAIAN RIFLES

HAMMERHEAD GUNSHIP

	Points	Armour:	Front	Side	Rear	BS
Hammerhead	90		13	12	10	3(4)

Type: Tank, Skimmer. **Crew:** Tau Fire caste.

Weapons: A Hammerhead is armed with a primary weapon system and a secondary weapon system.

The primary weapon system is either an ion cannon at +30 points or a railgun at +50 points.

The secondary weapon system is either two burst cannon at +10 points for the pair or a smart missile system at +20 points. Note that the burst cannon are not twin-linked and fire separately.

Options: The Hammerhead may be equipped with any of the vehicle upgrades permitted by the Tau Armoury. It is always equipped with a targeting array (already added to BS above) at no extra points cost.

The Hammerhead gunship is the main battle tank of the Tau army. Most of the internal space within the tank is taken up by capacitors for its weapon systems, and thus it cannot carry troops. During the Damocles Crusade, many Imperial tank crews learned the hard way how deadly its main weapons can be.

KROOTOX

	Points	WS	BS	S	T	W	I	A	Ld	Sv
Krootox	50	4	3	6	3(5)	3	3	3	*	*

Herd: A herd consists of 1-3 Krootox.

Equipment: Kroot gun.

SPECIAL RULES
Attached Unit: Krootox do not function as a separate unit on the tabletop. Although they occupy a Force Organisation chart Heavy Support choice, they must be attached to a Kroot Carnivore squad before the game.

They are then deployed along with the Kroot Carnivore squad as if they were all a Troops choice selection from the Force Organisation chart. There cannot be more models (counting Kroot Hounds and Krootox) added to a Carnivore squad than it initially consists of.

* Krootox, once attached, function as part of the Carnivore squad they are attached to. Their Leadership and Armour save will be the same as that of the Kroot unit they are attached to.

Note: *Krootox only have a Toughness of 3 for determining whether a weapon is capable of inflicting an instant kill, so weapons of Strength 6 or higher are able to kill them outright. In practice the hit will have killed the Kroot rider leaving the Krootox to wander off harmlessly. Remove the model as a casualty.*

Krootox are a divergent branch of Kroot evolution that lacked the qualities to become dominant. Krootox are ground-dwelling herbivores, far heavier than the normal Kroot. In battle, the Kroot lash large, unwieldy Kroot guns to their powerful shoulders and climb aboard its haunches, using the beast as a mobile weapon platform. Krootox are not aggressive creatures as a rule, but should an enemy attack their unit, they will fight ferociously to defend those they see as their herd brothers.

TAU SUMMARY

TAU, KROOT & DRONES STATISTICS

	WS	BS	S	T	W	I	A	Ld	Sv
Aun	4	3	3	3	2	3	3	10	-
Crisis Shas'o	4	5	5	4	4	3	4	10	3+
Crisis Shas'el	3	4	5	4	3	3	3	9	3+
Broadside Shas'vre	3	3	5	4	2	3	2	8	2+
Crisis Shas'vre	3	3	5	4	2	3	2	8	3+
Stealth Shas'vre	3	3	4	3	1	3	2	8	3+
Broadside Shas'ui	2	3	5	4	2	2	2	8	2+
Crisis Shas'ui	2	3	5	4	2	2	2	8	3+
Stealth Shas'ui	2	3	4	3	1	2	2	8	3+
Shas'ui	2	3	3	3	1	2	2	8	4+
Shas'la	2	3	3	3	1	2	1	7	4+
Shaper	4	3	4	3	3	3	3	7/8 *1	6+
Kroot	4	3	4	3	1	3	1	7/8 *1	*1
Kroot Hound	4	0	4	3	1	4	2	*1	*1
Krootox	4	3	6	3(5)	3	3	3	*1	*1
Gun Drone	2	2	3	3	1	4	1	7 *2	4+
Shield Drone	2	2	3	3	1	4	1	n/a	4+ *3

Tau Terminology

Aun are members of the Tau Ethereal caste.

Shas'la are basic Fire caste warriors.

Shas'ui are experienced Veterans who could potentially be equipped with a battlesuit.

Shas'vre are experienced battlesuit pilots.

Shas'el and Shas'o are force commanders.

The profiles left are adjusted to reflect the battlesuit enhancements possible to each rank of the Fire caste.

Notes

*1 Kroots' Leadership and Armour save is dependent on their points value.

*2 Gun Drones' Leadership is only applicable when operating in independent squadrons.

*3 Save is invulnerable.

*4 Kroot with Kroot rifles count as having an additional close combat weapon.

TAU VEHICLES STATISTICS

Vehicle / Armour:	Front	Side	Rear	BS
Devilfish Troop Carrier	12	11	10	3
Hammerhead Gunship	13	12	10	3(4)

TAU WEAPONS STATISTICS

Weapon	Range	Str	AP	Type	Notes
Burst cannon	18"	5	5	Assault 3	
Flamer	Template	4	5	Assault 1	
Fusion blaster	12"	8	1	Assault 1	2D6 Armour Pen. within 6"
Ion Cannon	60"	7	3	Heavy 3	
Kroot Gun	48"	7	4	Rapid Fire	
Kroot Rifle	24"	4	6	Rapid Fire	*4
Missile pod	36"	7	4	Assault 2	
Plasma rifle	24"	6	2	Rapid Fire	*Does not overheat*
Pulse Carbine	18"	5	5	Assault 1	*Pinning test*
Pulse Rifle	30"	5	5	Rapid Fire	
Railgun (solid shot)	72"	10	1	Heavy 1	
Railgun - submunition *(vehicle mounted only)*	72"	6	4	Heavy 1	*Ordnance blast*
Seeker Missile	*unlimited*	8	3	Heavy 1	*No line of sight needed Hits on 2+. Must be guided by a markerlight*
Smart Missile System	24"	5	5	Heavy 4	*No line of sight needed*

"It is not our technology that will enable us to prevail in this galaxy. It is our shared sense of honour and commonality of cause that unites us and will gives us the power to defeat our enemies."

SHAS'EL SA'CEA OR'ES, FIRE CASTE COMMANDER

Part of the attraction of collecting a Tau force is watching as it grows from a small cadre to a much larger army. From this force you can then expand your army to one capable of succeeding in any mission the Ethereals assign to it.

WHERE TO BEGIN?

The Tau army has a large and diverse selection of troops at its disposal, from Fire warriors, Kroot Carnivores and infiltrating Stealth armour teams to battlesuits capable of mounting potent heavy weaponry. Choosing which of these to take into battle can be a tough choice, as you'll no doubt want to pick all of them. However, the best thing to do first of all is to pick a 'core' force and then expand from there. That way you can quickly get your models on the table and be ready to play some games.

When you start collecting any force it is a good idea to keep in mind the Force Organisation charts printed in the Warhammer 40,000 rulebook. These charts dictate which unit types are available and how many of them you can field in battle. The best chart to look at first is the one for Standard Missions as this allows you to field a tactically flexible force which can quickly and easily be expanded at a later date.

As you can see from the chart below, a force chosen from the Standard Missions Force Organisation chart must have a minimum of at least one HQ unit and two Troops units, so it's a good idea to start collecting that first. Once you have this core force of one HQ unit and two units of Troops painted, you'll be ready to play some

games, although they'll be small ones at first. From here you can expand your army to play more varied scenarios and include some more specialised units. Each game you play will teach you more about how each unit works and what its particular strengths are.

The different elements of a Tau army need to work together to be successful, and as your army expands, you'll soon learn what works best for your style of play. Soon you'll have your full army and be ready to lead the glorious Tau empire to victory after victory in the name of the Greater Good.

A member of the Tau Ethereal Caste

A core Tau army force made up of two teams of Fire warriors (Troops) and a Fire warrior commander (HQ).

STANDARD MISSIONS

COMPULSORY	OPTIONAL
1 HQ	1 HQ
2 Troops	4 Troops
	3 Elites
	3 Fast Attack
	3 Heavy Support

HQ

ELITES

TROOPS — TROOPS — FAST ATTACK — HEAVY SUPPORT

On these pages you can see the different elements that make up a Tau army. Each part of the army has differing strengths and abilities, and a good commander recognises that every team has a specific role to play in battle, employing them where they will be most effective.

Ethereal caste member

Tau Commander & Crisis battlesuits

The mysterious Ethereal caste are the rulers of the Tau and their presence inspires the Fire warriors to heroic acts of valour. Tau forces are most often led by a Fire warrior Commander who will frequently be accompanied by a bodyguard of Fire warriors clad in XV8 Crisis battlesuits. Together with the commander, these warriors form an HQ unit on the battlefield and are capable of mounting an array of deadly weaponry that can meet almost any threat and neutralise it. Crisis battlesuits may also be fielded as Elite units, able to act independently on the battlefield.

Fire warriors

Fire warriors are the basic Troop type of the Tau forces, and you must include at least one unit in your army. Though they are neither especially tough or strong, their pulse rifles and carbines are ideal defensive weapons, capable of laying down a withering salvo of fire that can pin the enemy in place for heavier units to engage. Fire warrior teams can also be mounted in a Devilfish Troop Carrier to speed their deployment.

The mercenary Kroot can be fielded as a Troop choice in a Tau army and provide it with some fearsome close combat warriors. They fight with long rifles, equipped with lethal close combat blades, though some Kroot can carry more hi-tech weaponry. Vicious Kroot Hounds run alongside their handlers, ready to pursue a defeated foe and the lumbering Krootox carries the powerful Kroot gun with which to give the Carnivore squads some heavy fire support.

Kroot Carnivores with Kroot Hounds & Krootox

Pathfinders with Devilfish Troop Carrier

Pathfinders are the forward scouts of a Tau force and are able to work themselves into prime spotting positions where they can use their Markerlights to enable those carrying heavier weapons to shoot with pinpoint accuracy. Pathfinders are always mounted in a Devilfish Troop Carrier and this enables them to rapidly redeploy should their position be compromised.

Broadside battlesuits

Tau gun drones

The largest battlesuits in the Tau army, Broadsides fill a Heavy Support slot on the Force Organisation Chart. They are best employed in commanding positions where their devastating heavy weaponry can engage the greatest number of targets. Nothing is safe from the Broadsides' weapons, from the heaviest tank to well dug-in infantry and, if equipped with a missile system, they can even engage targets they cannot see.

Gun drones may be networked together to form separate units on the battlefield and taken as a Fast Attack choice. They are ideal for supporting other units and sneaking around the flanks of the enemy, using their twin-linked pulse carbines to pin enemy units in place.

Hammerhead gunship

Stealth battlesuits

The Hammerhead is a fearsome tank, easily the equal of any Imperial vehicle, and its rail gun makes light of even the thickest armour. Hammerheads substitute transport capacity in order to carry an array of deadly weapons and are ideal for destroying enemy vehicles.

Powerful holographic disruption fields allow Stealth teams to sneak forward unobserved into advantageous firing positions before battle commences. They are hard to detect and their burst cannons are the perfect weapons for ambushing lightly armoured troops and attacking the flanks of vehicles.

EXPANDING THE FORCE

Once you have your two Troop choices and one HQ choice you'll want to begin expanding your army. A convenient way of doing this is to choose a selection from each of the other categories in the Force Organisation chart.

THE ARMY GROWS

Having painted your core force and played a few games, you'll be wanting to expand your army and fight some bigger battles. There are a lot of troop types to choose from in the Tau list and all have their particular strengths. In this section, we'll give you some guidance about the best way to enlarge your Tau army.

Many gamers like to make sure their force expands in a balanced way by selecting a choice from each of the categories on the Force Organisation chart, Elites, Fast Attack and Heavy Support. This way your army grows quickly and you retain a flexible force capable of holding its own against whatever mission or army you find yourself facing.

You might decide to take a team of Stealth battlesuits, some Pathfinders and a team of Broadside battlesuits. This gives you a hard-hitting force capable of springing a surprise attack from hiding and a selection of heavy weapons whose accuracy can be enhanced by the

Pathfinders' Markerlights. Or you may decide you prefer the sight of armoured vehicles and take Devilfish Troop Carriers or a Hammerhead gunship.

The Tau are equipped with some of the most effective weaponry in the galaxy and they work best by keeping the enemy at arm's length. Even a basic Fire warrior's weapon delivers a powerful hit, and the larger guns can tear even the most heavily armoured foe apart. The Tau consider close combat a brutish affair best left to those with a genuine skill for it, and should things threaten to get up close and personal, the Tau can call upon the Kroot, their mercenary allies. These aliens are fearsome fighters and excel in the fury of close combat.

The way you prefer to fight your battles will play a large part in your selections, and after a few games, you'll soon discover what works best for you. Whatever style of play you favour, the Tau army can be configured to fight in that manner so it's completely up to you how you use it.

The original core force has been expanded to include a Crisis Battlesuit team (Elite), a Hammerhead gunship (Heavy Support), and a Pathfinder team (Fast Attack).

TAU TACTICS

Once you have your army, you'll want to fight and win with it. Learning how to use your army well is part of the pleasure of playing Warhammer 40,000 and to help you further the expansion of the Tau empire, we'll impart the wisdom of previous Fire caste Commanders.

Kauyon (Patient Hunter): The Tau army is at its best when engaging the enemy at long range. Tau tactics are therefore focused on getting the enemy in clear view so that the Tau shooting can be decisive. The Kauyon method does this by using a lure to tempt the enemy forward. In this photo a Tau army has set up to perform a Kauyon using the Stealth team as the lure.

The Hammerhead Gunship, Commander and Crisis team wait for the enemy to be drawn into attacking the Stealth team.

The Broadside team are in covering positions and are armed with smart missile systems so they can provide supporting fire while out of sight of the enemy.

Fire warriors form a line which can be reinforced by the reserve if required. The Devilfish is placed for quick embarkation if needed.

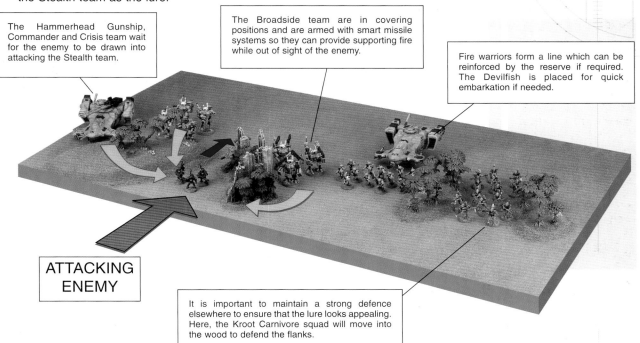

ATTACKING ENEMY

It is important to maintain a strong defence elsewhere to ensure that the lure looks appealing. Here, the Kroot Carnivore squad will move into the wood to defend the flanks.

Mont'ka (Killing Blow): It is not always necessary to wait for the enemy to rush into your gunsights to apply firepower. Mont'ka is about swiftly deploying your firepower so that a portion of the enemy army is quickly overwhelmed. This photo shows a Tau army set up to execute the Mont'ka with their mobile troops while using the Kroot squad and Broadside team to support them when they act.

The Broadsides are deployed amongst the Kroot. When the Mont'ka is executed, the Broadsides will move forward to engage the enemy.

The hill is being used by the Commander, Crisis team and Hammerhead to provide them with cover from the enemy until they strike.

The Fire warriors will manoeuvre to put the enemy in doubt about the overall plan.

The Kroot are deployed so that they can move into the cover of the wood. They support the Tau and prevent the flank being turned.

TAU CONSTRUCTION TIPS

The bulk of your army will be made up of plastic kits and you can achieve a wide variety of poses from the different arm, weapon and wargear configurations available. On this page we'll give you some tips on getting the most from your models.

FIRE WARRIOR CONSTRUCTION TIPS

Glue the aerial in place first

Shoulder pad right way up

Glue the legs to the base then stick the torso on. Glue the backpack on and stick the aerial to the helmet, since it's less awkward to get it in place at this stage. A handy tip is to use Blu-tac to make sure you're happy with the positioning of your models before you glue them.

Fire warriors' arms are paired up on the frame, so when you cut one from the frame, cut the opposite arm off as well. Glue the arms on and fit the shoulder guard to the left arm with the sept symbol to the top. With the gun in position you can now glue the head on.

You can also assemble the models carrying specialised equipment. The frame allows you to fit a variant arm carrying either a grenade or sensor equipment. If you use either of these arms, use one of the weaponless arms to carry a gun.

KROOT CONSTRUCTION TIPS

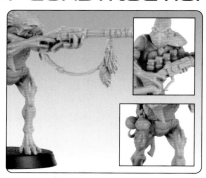

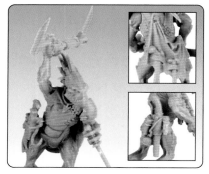

Glue the torso and legs together and fix them to the base, then stick the model's arms to the torso. Remember to position the arms in such a way that allows you to fix chest accessories later.

The frame allows you to attach various accessories to the model such as knives, pistols, hooks, etc, so leave areas free for them. Slings can be attached to the weapons and shoulder guards to the arms.

To provide variety to your Kroot squads, you can use the heads bearing jewellery incorporated into the quills, and the knife arm. This enables you to add fearsome accessories such as the rack of ribs and bone cape.

BATTLESUIT CONSTRUCTION TIPS

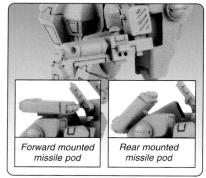

Forward mounted missile pod

Rear mounted missile pod

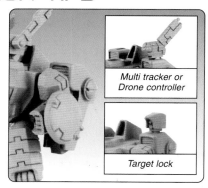

Multi tracker or Drone controller

Target lock

Glue the body together and decide whether the model is standing or flying. If you want the model on the ground, glue the feet flat on a 40mm base (You can use Blu tac to ensure the feet fit the angle of the legs before you glue them). If the model is using his jetpack, use a flying base and angle the feet downwards.

Fit the weapons into the grooves on the arms before gluing them to the model. The weapons can be mounted on either the arms or shoulders. The missile pod looks great on the shoulder mount and you can alter the dynamic of the model by changing the angle of the missile pod as shown above.

You can equip Tau battlesuits with various items of wargear, and these are best positioned on the shoulder mounts, although the shield generator looks great on the arm. Once you've attached any shoulder mounted weapons or wargear you can glue the model's head to the body, remembering to stick the aerial on first.

PAINTING FIRE WARRIORS

This section guides you through the various stages we used to paint our Tau army. We'll show you how you can paint your Fire warriors, using a number of simple techniques that will enable you to assemble a painted, battle ready force. Remember that there's no right or wrong way to paint, pick whichever method works best for you.

1.

First of all we undercoated this Fire warrior using a spray can of Chaos Black then painted his armour and weapon with Vermin Brown. The cloth of the undersuit was painted in a 50/50 mix of Scorched Brown and Chaos Black.

2.

With the base colours painted we then used Vomit Brown as the main colour for the armour and Scorched Brown for the cloth of the undersuit. Using contrasting colours is a good way to make both colours really stand out.

3.

To finish off the Fire warrior, we used a final highlight of Bleached Bone along the edges of the armour panels and painted the Tau symbol on his shoulder guard. This model is also equipped with a Ta'lissera bonding knife, fixed to his back.

PAINTING TECHNIQUES

Drybrushing is a technique you can use to highlight your models, especially textured and metal parts. While it's a quicker method of highlighting, the quality of finish isn't as good as the techniques described above. Dip the brush in the colour you want to highlight with and then wipe away most of the paint from the bristles with a tissue. Then lightly draw the brush over the model, catching the raised areas with the highlighting colour.

Ink washes are used to quickly shade your models. Using a slightly darker colour ink than the model's base coat, brush a light wash of ink over the model and allow it to seep into the recesses. This will give the model a rich, shading effect and once this ink wash is dry you can drybrush the raised areas of the model to apply the highlights. Be careful not to use too much ink as they can take quite a while to dry.

BASES

Apply PVA glue to the model's base and sprinkle on some sand. Paint it Bestial Brown and drybrush with Bleached Bone. Paint the edges of the base with Goblin Green and when everything is dry, dab a few dots of PVA onto the base and sprinkle on some flock or static grass to add the finishing touch.

ETHEREALS & TAU FLESH

Dave Thomas

When Dave Thomas painted this Tau Ethereal, he painted the flesh of the model using a base colour of Shadow Grey. He then used a 50/50 mix of Elf Flesh and Shadow Grey for the main colour. The final highlights on the skin were added by using Ghostly Grey. It's worth spending a little extra time to think of how you want Ethereals to look before you start painting as these are the most revered individuals in Tau society and should look suitably regal and important. A nicely painted model will really stand out on the table top, and the Ethereals also give you an opportunity to paint Tau skin.

The elite units of a Tau army are its battlesuits, and they form an impressive centrepiece to your army. As such, they will really benefit from the best paint job you can give them and here we show you how you can achieve impressive results painting your models with some basic techniques.

After spraying the models with Chaos Black the armour's base colour was painted with Vermin Brown. The helmet's colour was achieved with a 50/50 mix of Vermin Brown and Vomit Brown.

The armour was then painted with Vomit Brown and the helmet with a 75/25 mix of Skull White and Vomit Brown. The rest of the model was painted with a 50/50 mix of Codex Grey and Chaos Black, leaving the recesses black. To add a little variety to the model, you can paint the odd panel in a 50/50 mix of Scab Red and Scorched Brown.

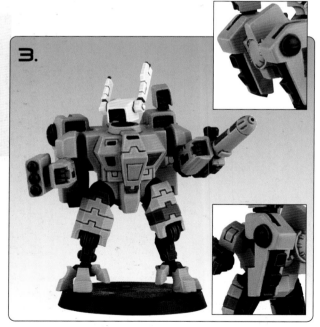

Highlights were added to the armour with Bronzed Flesh and to the helmet with Skull White. The darker areas such as the exhaust outlets and lower legs were given a final highlight of Codex Grey. The panels painted in red had a little Bleached Bone added to the mix to lighten the edges.

All that remains is to add the final details to the model. The upper edges of the armour and helmet were given a final highlight of Bleached Bone. The optic on the helmet was painted with Red Gore and lightened with Blood Red and Blazing Orange, with a final highlight added by painting on a dot of Skull White. The sept marking was applied with a transfer, as was the Ta'lissera dagger symbol on the chest plate and team markings were then added to the weapons. With the detailing done, we then based the model using the same techniques mentioned before.

Tau Broadside battlesuit

Tau Stealth battlesuit

This Stealth warrior was painted in darker tones as befits the nature of his battlefield role. We painted the undersuit Scorched Brown and highlighted it by adding some Bleached Bone. The dark red armour plates were painted with a 50/50 mix of Scab Red and Scorched Brown then highlighted by adding Bleached Bone to the mix. The cannon and shoulder guards were painted with a 50/50 mix of Chaos Black and Codex Grey then highlighted with Codex Grey along the edges. If you have a steady hand, a further highlight can be added by painting a very thin line of Fortress Grey along the edges. This same technique was used on the black areas of the adjacent Broadside battlesuit's weapons.

Tau battlesuits

PAINTING TAU VEHICLES

Tau vehicles can be painted very quickly, no matter how complex they might look at first. In this section we'll show you how to paint your vehicles with techniques you can apply to both the Hammerhead Gunship and the Devilfish Troop Carrier.

Hammerhead Gunship with railgun

After undercoating the vehicles with Chaos Black, they were painted in several thinned down coats of Vomit Brown to provide even coverage over the model. To give them a clean, precise feel, thin strips of Vermin Brown were painted into the panel lines. To break up the uniformly coloured areas, some panels were painted in a 50/50 mix of Scab Red and Scorched Brown. Dark areas such as the weapon mount and exhausts were highlighted using the same method as described for the Stealth warriors. Highlights to the hull were applied using Bleached Bone.

STIPPLING

The 'Eavy Metal team used a technique known as 'stippling' to achieve the desert camouflage look of the vehicles. To do this, use a brush that's near the end of its life and put some Vermin Brown on it. Wipe most of the paint from the bristles, making sure there's hardly any paint left on the brush, and then dab it lightly over the flat surfaces of the vehicle in small, circular motions.

Devilfish Troop Carrier

It's a good idea to paint the Tau crewman separately from the tank, to ensure that you can get to all the hard to reach areas before you glue him in place.

Here, the exhaust fairings have been painted to look weathered by using the 'stippling' technique with Scorched Brown. A further layer of stippling was then applied with some Chaos Black added to the mix to darken the colouring.

Remember to remove the vehicle's gun drones and paint them separately, otherwise you'll expose a large unpainted area of your model if you decide to detach them during a game!

TAU MARKINGS

The sept a Tau comes from is an important part of who he is. It forms part of his name and carries a number of subtle meanings. It is therefore important that each warrior bears the symbol of the sept he hails from. On this page, we'll show you how you can easily apply these markings to your Fire warriors, battlesuits and vehicles.

TRANSFERS

Transfers are a simple way to apply sept markings to your models. Cut the sept marking you want from the transfer sheet and dip it in a saucer of water for about thirty seconds. Then, using a pair of tweezers and a brush, slide the design from the backing paper onto the model.

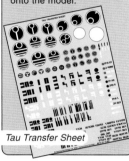

Tau Transfer Sheet

We painted the Tau leaders' helmets a different colour to distinguish them from their team. We gave Shas'ui and Shas'vre team leaders pale helmets and Commanders red helmets, though you can invent your own colour schemes.

Battlesuits bear sept markings on shield plates on their back and have a number of different markings on their armour. Team markings can be painted on the armour or weapons and it doesn't matter which so long as you stay consistent within the team. Teams that have been bonded by a Ta'lissera ritual will bear the dagger symbol on the left chest plate of their armour and battlesuits often have warning symbols around the edges of their jet packs exhausts. Individual team members frequently bear their own markings across their helmet aerials also.

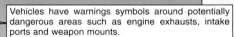

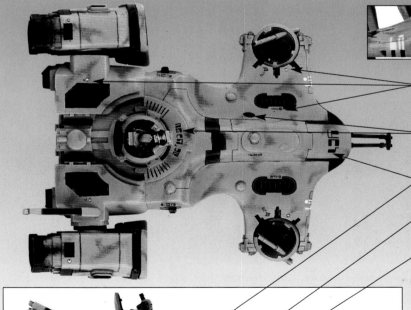

Vehicles have warnings symbols around potentially dangerous areas such as engine exhausts, intake ports and weapon mounts.

It is common for the Fire warrior tank commander to have his own name around the turret ring and his personal marking on the vehicle side.

Each vehicle's number is shown on its frontal section and sides, with the side numbers smaller than the frontal ones.

Tau vehicles display the sept the crew are from on the side doors and rear crew ramp.

Tau vehicles often sport army badges and Tau slogans that exhort the troops in the name of the Greater Good!

FIRE WARRIORS

Fire warriors always bear the symbol of the Tau home world on the shoulder guard of their left arm. We've also chosen to paint team markings around the barrel of their rifles and on the edge of their helmets, but you can paint these anywhere you like.

Tau team leader

TAU COLOUR SCHEMES

Tau armies have many varying colour schemes, and on this page you can see some of the different ones the 'Eavy Metal team came up with. You can use these as they are for your own army or as inspiration for inventing your own colour scheme.

Each Tau sept has different colour scheme and, while this is recognised as that particular sept's colours, an army from that sept does not always have to be fielded in these colours. You can invent your own colour scheme for your army or find inspiration in lots of different places, from movies, history books or even other Codexes.

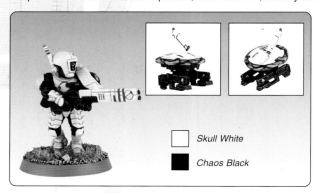

Skull White
Chaos Black

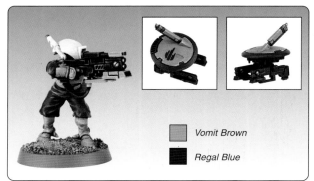

Vomit Brown
Regal Blue

Camo Green
Dark Angels Green

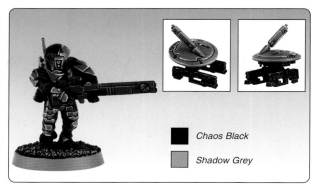

Chaos Black
Shadow Grey

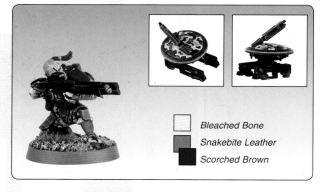

Bleached Bone
Snakebite Leather
Scorched Brown

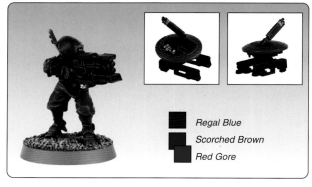

Regal Blue
Scorched Brown
Red Gore

Hawk Turquoise
Skull White
Scorched Brown
Bleached Bone

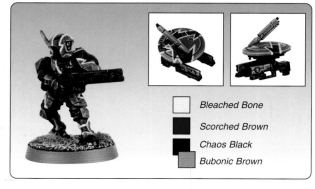

Bleached Bone
Scorched Brown
Chaos Black
Bubonic Brown

TAU TERRAIN

There's nothing quite as impressive as a fully modelled battlefield to play your games of Warhammer 40,000 over and, while most terrain is suitable for any army, a themed battlefield is much more visually exciting. Adding terrain to match your army is a good way of making your battles much more involving.

The famous Ethereal, Aun'shi, led the heroic defence of the Tau outpost of Fio'vash when it came under attack from hordes of Orks.

During the Nimbosa Annexation, Tau forces were able to throw the 33rd Cadians into disarray by springing carefully prepared ambushes then falling back to landing platforms for their Devilfish Troop Carriers.

Examples of materials that Mark used for terrain in its raw state (plant pots, etc)

Mark Jones

Studio Model Maker, Mark Jones, constructed both these Tau terrain pieces using a number of different materials. Upturned flowerpots served as a base for the building and landing platform, then Mark used a mixture of specially cast resins, plasticard and spare drones from the Fire warrior plastic kits to build up the details. The Tau symbol is a recurring motif as is the use of domed shapes. Most of the materials used by Mark can be found at hobby shops, garden centres or by raiding your bits box.

PAINTING KROOT

The Kroot give you the opportunity to achieve a very different look to part of your army. Although the Kroot are unlike the Tau, you can use exactly the same techniques to achieve impressive results and on this page we'll show you how.

1.

2.

3.

The Kroot were sprayed with Chaos Black then we used a 50/50 mix of Scorched Brown and Camo Green to paint on the base coat. The quills on the Kroot's head were painted with Leprous Brown and the leather and rifle stock were painted with Dark Flesh. For the metallic parts of the rifle we used Boltgun Metal.

Some Rotting Flesh was added to the mix to paint on the Kroot's main skin colour. To add highlights to the leather we painted on some Vermin Brown and for the rifle stock used Bestial Brown. To highlight the rifle we used Mithril Silver.

Final highlights were added by using Rotting Flesh for the skin and Bleached Bone for the quills. The leather was finished with a mix of Vermin Brown and Bleached Bone. To finish the stock, we used a 50/50 mix of Scorched Brown and Bleached Bone.

DRYBRUSHING KROOT

The Kroot are an element of your army that really suit drybrushing. Skin tones and flesh can be quickly highlighted as the raised areas of muscle on the Kroot models are ideal for catching the paint as you apply the drybrushing.

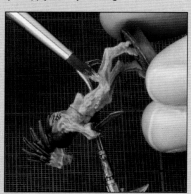

PAINTING KROOTOX & KROOT HOUNDS

For the Krootox, Tammy Haye painted the skin with a mix of Chaos Black, Scorched Brown and Goblin Green. Then, each highlight was built up with progressively more Rotting Flesh added to the mix. The eyes were painted in Bleached Bone and highlighted with Skull White. Coloured excretions on the Krootoxs skin were added with a Red Gore/Dark Flesh mix and a wash of Red Ink. A thinned down mix of Green, Black and Brown ink was used as a final glaze over the Krootox skin to blend the colours smoothly together. As these creatures are evolutionary cousins to the Kroot, the techniques you'll use to paint them aren't much different. We painted these models using the same techniques, but used differing skin tones to further differentiate the various creatures. The heavier Krootox was painted a darker shade, while the Kroot Hounds were painted a lighter shade, using the same colours and techniques as the Kroot themselves.

Tammy Haye

KROOT COLOUR SCHEMES

The Kroot can be almost any colour imaginable, from earthy tones to vivid and striking colours that really stand out. There's no limit to the colours you can choose for Kroot and on this page you can see some of the colour variations we tried.

The unique Kroot digestive system allows them to alter their skin pigmentation radically in response to absorbed DNA and thus Kroot from different kindreds are often identifiable by the colour of their skin and quills. Kroot also frequently mark themselves by secreting an oily sweat that colours the desired areas of their skin and these are another way of recognising Kroot from different kindreds. This allows you to paint your Kroot in all manner of different colour schemes.

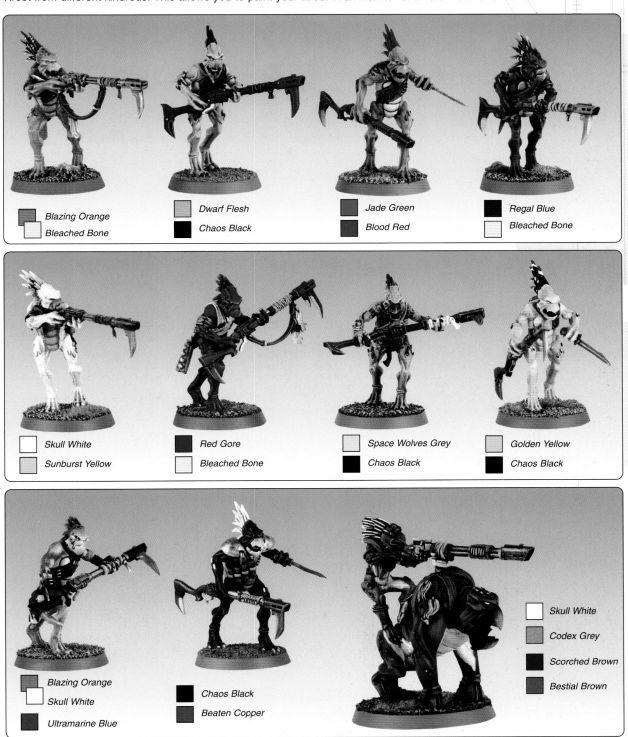

Blazing Orange
Bleached Bone

Dwarf Flesh
Chaos Black

Jade Green
Blood Red

Regal Blue
Bleached Bone

Skull White
Sunburst Yellow

Red Gore
Bleached Bone

Space Wolves Grey
Chaos Black

Golden Yellow
Chaos Black

Blazing Orange
Skull White
Ultramarine Blue

Chaos Black
Beaten Copper

Skull White
Codex Grey
Scorched Brown
Bestial Brown

SHOWCASE

On this page you can see some of the best examples of Tau and Kroot models painted by the 'Eavy Metal team. Well painted models make an impressive addition to any army and hopefully these will inspire you in your own painting.

Legendary Kroot Shaper, Anghkor Prok by Tammy Haye

Stealth battlesuit by Martin Footitt

Tau Fire warrior by Keith Robertson

Kroot Shaper by Martin Footitt

Devilfish and Pathfinders by Keith Robertson

Renegade Fire caste commander O'Shovah by Kirsten Williams

The famous Tau Ethereal, Aun'shi, by Tammy Haye

Laeresh carefully scanned the moonlit trees before the Ranger squad, the muzzle of her long rifle following the movement of her eyes. Her every sense was attuned to the rhythm of the forest, alert for something out of place, something alien. Nothing disturbed the quiet save the ordinary sounds of animal life she had come to expect. Had any of their enemies been nearby, the native creatures would have fled, or given some other warning of their presence. Satisfied, she lowered the rifle and lifted her right fist, the fingers spread, the sign that all was well. Laeresh returned the rifle to her shoulder, soundlessly rising from the crouch and crept forwards, each step carefully placed as she advanced through the trees.

The five Eldar Rangers moved like ghosts as they worked their way forwards, Cameleoline cloaks shifting in hue until the Eldar scouts were all but invisible. Laeresh stalked silently towards a wide-trunked vinetree.

Then all hell broke loose.

Laeresh spun as a Kroot dropped from the trees behind her. The powerful alien reared over her, shaking the quills on the back of its head and hissing a challenge. She twisted, bringing her rifle to bear, but the enormous Kroot swung the blade attached to his primitive firearm up and hacked through the barrel as she pressed the firing stud. The rifle's charging chamber exploded in a searing white fireball and Laeresh fell, burnt and half-blinded. Most of the Kroot's head had been blasted away and it toppled forwards, pinning her against the tree. Dancing motes of light, afterimages seared onto her retina, burst before her and she blinked furiously, simultaneously trying to clear her vision and push the dead Kroot away.

The night echoed with screams as more Kroot burst from hiding and leapt upon the Eldar scouts. Laeresh saw her cousin Culiern defend himself from two Kroot and screamed his name as a third drove a blade through his back, the tip bursting from his chest in a spray of blood. She watched Finugal and Duatha drop their long rifles and draw their shuriken pistols as Medhar was bludgeoned to death. Now it was the Kroot's turn to die as the air was filled with deadly, razor-edged projectiles, slicing through their alien flesh with ease. For a moment Laeresh dared hope they might live through this until Duatha's head was ripped from her shoulders by the powerful hands of a Kroot warrior. Finugal spun to face the leader of the Kroot and fired his pistol at point blank range, the monomolecular discs tearing through its side. The alien took no notice and Finugal was lifted high into the air as the Kroot slammed the bladed butt of his rifle into his belly. Laeresh wept as Finugal was held suspended, screaming as blood fountained from his body. The Kroot wrapped a hand around his victim's neck and wrenched the blade from the body. He pulled the dying Eldar close and tore a bloody chunk of flesh from his neck with his powerful, beaked jaws.

Laeresh tried to work her hand down to her holster as the horrifying sound of the Kroot feasting on her friends reached her. Bones snapped as the Kroot tore their victims apart, devouring the still-warm organs within. Her hand closed on the smooth grip of her pistol. She drew and fired in one motion, almost beheading one of the bloodstained Kroot. A backhanded blow knocked the pistol flying and a rifle butt slammed into her face, blood filling her mouth. Dazed, she felt herself being dragged out from beneath the dead Kroot, hearing the clicking, whistling language of her captors. Her limbs were seized in vice-like grips, holding her immobile. She screamed as she felt the Kroot fasten their jaws on her leg and begin feeding.

She was still alive as the Kroot broke her ribcage open. The Kroot leader devouring her heart was the last thing Laeresh ever saw.

O'shovah, or Commander Farsight, is alleged to still lead the Farsight enclave, although this would mean that he has lived for at least three centuries, considerably beyond the ordinary lifespan of the Tau Fire caste. It may be that another has taken up his mantle, or that the real Commander is extending his lifespan through some technological process. One thing that is certain is that the breakaway Farsight enclave maintains a strongly martial tradition closely based on the Vior'la sept (lit: 'hot-blooded'), O'shovah's birthplace.

COMMANDER FARSIGHT (TAU: O'SHOVAH OR SHAS'O VIOR'LA SHOVAH KAIUS MONT'YR)

	WS	BS	S	T	W	I	A	Ld	Sv	Points
Farsight	5	5	3(5)	3(4)	3(4)	5	4	10	3+	170

Special Character: A Tau army may include Commander Farsight as a special character. If you decide to take him then he counts as one of the HQ choices for the army. He must be used exactly as described below and may not be given extra equipment from the Tau Armoury.

Equipment: XV8 Crisis battlesuit, shield generator, plasma rifle and Dawn Blade (see below).

SPECIAL RULES:

Dawn Blade: The Dawn Blade is an alien artefact which O'shovah gained on the dead world of Arthas-Moloch. Its sculpted surface flickers with unknown energies which paint glittering arcs of destruction as it is swung. The Dawn Blade makes O'shovah count as a Monstrous Creature in hand-to-hand combat, so he ignores Armour saves and rolls 2D6+5 for Armour Penetration against vehicles.

Ork Fighter: O'shovah's fame was won battling against Orks, and he has denounced the normal Tau philosophy of using ranged combat to the exclusion of almost all else. Fire caste warriors of the Farsight enclave train heavily in hand-to-hand combat, and any Tau unit in an army led by O'shovah may improve both their WS and I characteristics by 1, at a cost of +5 points per model.

Breakaway Faction: O'shovah and his followers have chosen to separate themselves from the Tau empire. As such, their resources are more limited and their forces generally less well equipped. As such, the following units are not available to an army led by O'shovah: Ethereal caste members, Gun Drone squadrons, Kroot, Kroot Hounds and Krootox. The following units count as 0-1 in an army led by O'shovah: Stealth teams, Pathfinder teams, Hammerhead gunships, Broadside Battlesuit teams.

Independent Character: Unless accompanied by a bodyguard, O'shovah is an independent character and follows all the independent character special rules as detailed in the Warhammer 40,000 rulebook.

Bodyguard. O'shovah may be accompanied by a bodyguard as detailed for a Commander in the Codex army list. If O'shovah is accompanied by a bodyguard, they must all be given the Ork Fighter upgrade noted above

THE ARKUNASHA WAR

O'shovah's first and greatest victories were won amid the arid oxide-deserts of Arkunasha. When the Tau colony there was threatened, he led the Fire warriors in a masterful defence against many times their own numbers. Using the immense canyons and gulleys criss-crossing the desert to maximum effect, O'shovah set the Ork invaders to chase shadows, constantly boxing off and destroying isolated elements wherever they turned at bay, earning him the famous title 'Farsight' for his actions. It is true that towards the end of the war O'shovah was in turn surrounded and besieged by massive numbers of Orks in the natural fortress of the Argap highlands, but even then his Fire warriors held the mountains for months until the last remnants were evacuated. Some believe that the Commander was embittered by the bloodshed of siege and blamed others for failing to break through the encirclement. Instead the Orks were allowed to batter themselves to a standstill against O'shovah's defences before being easily scattered the following year.

COMMIT TO: IMPERIAL RECORD
EST 02/8301 INQUISITORIA 8953/3932
CROSSFILE TO: ALIENS
EASTERN FRINGE
MERCENARIES
TAU
INPUT DATE: 6284996M41
INPUT CLEARANCE: INQUISITOR ARTELLES
AUTHOR: AGENT OSSNEOUS
TRANSMITTED: VANGOR IX
TRANSMITTER: ASTROPATH PRIMUS TIEN'SZAR
THOUGHT FOR THE DAY:
PURE IN BODY, PURE IN HEART.

HONOURED SIR, AS REQUESTED I HAVE INVESTIGATED THE RUMOURS OF A BREAKAWAY SECTION OF THE TAU EMPIRE, AND THE OPERATIONS OF TAU MERCENARY FORCES IN THE HORST SECTOR AND DAMOCLES GULF. AS YOU POSTULATED, THESE TWO STORIES HAVE THE SAME ROOT, REVOLVING AROUND AN INFLUENTIAL FIRE CASTE COMMANDER CALLED O'SHOVAH, OR COMMANDER FARSIGHT, WHO APPEARS TO HAVE SPLIT OFF FROM THE MAINSTREAM TAU CULTURE. AS YOU WILL BE AWARE, THE TAU EMPIRE HAS TO DATE BEEN THOUGHT EXCEEDINGLY COHESIVE WITH NO DISSIDENT ELEMENTS AND, AS SUCH, THIS EVIDENCE IS PARTICULARLY INTRIGUING AS IT REPRESENTS THE FIRST KNOWN INCIDENCE OF TAU TREASON OR HERESY.

INTENSIVE QUESTIONING OF CHARTER MERCHANTS AND FREE CAPTAINS HAS UNCOVERED SOME INFORMATION, ALTHOUGH THE COMPLETE PICTURE REMAINS RATHER MURKY. IT APPEARS THAT AFTER THE HALT OF THE DAMOCLES CRUSADE, WHEN OUR SHIPS WERE CALLED TO THE DEFENCE AGAINST HIVE FLEET BEHEMOTH, SEVERAL TAU RECLAMATION FORCES WERE DESPATCHED TO RECONQUER THEIR LOST COLONIES. O'SHOVAH WAS THE LEADER OF ONE SUCH FORCE, A CONSIDERABLE FLEET OF SHIPS AND GROUND TROOPS ACCOMPANYING COLONY SHIPS TO REPOPULATE THE CLEANSED WORLDS. AS IS CUSTOMARY, ONE OR MORE TAU ETHEREAL CASTE MEMBERS WERE ALSO PART OF THE EXPEDITION. IT APPEARS THAT COMMANDER FARSIGHT'S EXPEDITION RAN INTO UNEXPECTED DIFFICULTIES WITH AN ORK INCURSION PROBING AT THE SHATTERED EDGES OF THE TAU EMPIRE. O'SHOVAH ABANDONED HIS RECOLONISATION MISSION AND INSTEAD DIRECTED HIS EFFORTS AT FIGHTING THE ORKS AND WAS DRAWN INTO A DECADE-LONG CAMPAIGN ACROSS MANY WORLDS.

IN TIME, O'SHOVAH'S FORCES PUSHED BACK INTO SEVERAL ORK HELD SYSTEMS IN THE DAMOCLES GULF AND INFLICTED EXTERMINATUS UPON THEIR WORLDS, EFFECTIVELY TERMINATING THE IMMEDIATE THREAT. BY NOW THE EXPEDITION WAS WELL BEYOND THE KNOWN REACHES OF TAU SPACE AND IT SEEMS THAT O'SHOVAH CHOSE TO ESTABLISH A STRING OF HEAVILY FORTIFIED STRONGHOLD-COLONIES IN THE REGION INSTEAD OF RETURNING TO THE EMPIRE. BY OUR RECKONING THIS WOULD BE SOMETIME AROUND 760.M41 BUT AN ACCURATE PROJECTION IS IMPOSSIBLE WITH CURRENT FACTS. I HAVE THE FIRST REPORT OF ALIEN MERCENARIES WHICH WOULD FIT THE DESCRIPTION OF TAU FIRE WARRIORS FIGHTING ALONGSIDE PIRATE FORCES IN THE SACK OF PENURY IV 7330763.M41. RUMOURS OF SUCH ACTIVITY CROP UP THROUGHOUT THE PERIOD 770-820 BEFORE DROPPING AWAY NOTICEABLY TO OCCASIONAL REPORTS UP TO THE PRESENT. IF SUCH RUMOURS ARE TO BE BELIEVED (WHICH MUST BE DONE WITH NATURAL CAUTION), THESE TAU MERCENARIES HAVE FOUGHT ALONGSIDE KROOT (UNSURPRISINGLY), TARELLIANS, HUMAN RENEGADES, ELDAR, THE ACCURSED TRAITOR LEGIONS AND EVEN ORKS. OUR MOST SOLID PIECE OF INFORMATION IS THE OFFER OF ASSISTANCE REPORTED BY PREFECT VERTEX IN THE EVACUATION OF ALEPH SIGMA 5664994.M41 IN THE FACE OF ONE OF THE TYRANID SPLINTER-FLEETS FROM ICHAR IV — HIVE FLEET HARBINGER I BELIEVE. I SUSPECT THAT A NUMBER OF FREE CAPTAINS HAVE ESTABLISHED TRADE ROUTES INTO THE FARSIGHT ENCLAVES, BUT THEY REMAIN CLOSE-MOUTHED ABOUT THE SUBJECT. I HAVE NOT PURSUED SUCH MATTERS FURTHER IN FEAR OF SCARING THESE INDIVIDUALS AWAY AT A TIME WHEN WE MAY NEED TO ELICIT THEIR ASSISTANCE TO FIND OUT MORE.

OF THE APPARENT INTENTIONS OF O'SHOVAH, IF HE STILL LIVES, I CANNOT SAY. THE CIRCUMSTANCES OF HIS BREAKAWAY FROM THE TAU EMPIRE REMAIN SHROUDED IN MYSTERIES SO PERSISTENT THAT I STRONGLY SUSPECT THAT THEY ARE BEING MANIPULATED BY SOME AGENCY IN ORDER TO HIDE THE TRUTH. THE ONE CLUE I COULD UNCOVER IN THIS DIRECTION WAS BROUGHT TO ME BY A CERTAIN FREE CAPTAIN DALMUERTUS WHO ACTIVELY SOUGHT ME OUT AND SEEMED GENUINELY CONCERNED BY WHAT HE'D HEARD. I HAVE INCLUDED A TRANSCRIPT OF THE STORY HE TOLD ME VERBATIM SO THAT YOU MAY MAKE YOUR OWN JUDGEMENT OF IT. I WOULD STRONGLY URGE THAT STEPS BE UNDERTAKEN TO INFILTRATE THIS TAU ENCLAVE AND DISCOVER WHAT CONDITIONS ARE TRULY LIKE THERE. IF CAPTAIN DALMUERTUS' TESTIMONY PROVES TRUE IT MAY INDICATE THAT O'SHOVAH HAS BEEN CORRUPTED IN SOME WAY ON THE ARTEFACT WORLD REFERRED TO. IF THIS IS TRUE THEN THERE IS A GREATER THREAT GROWING IN THE FARSIGHT STRONGHOLDS THAN THAT REPRESENTED BY THE ENTIRE TAU EMPIRE.

YOUR DEVOTED SERVANT

OSSNEOUS

CAPT DALMUERTUS' TESTIMONY

+ + + + BEGIN VOX RECORD + + + + +

"WELL, SEE I HAVE CONTACTS WITH THE TAU, AND FOR XENOS THEY TREAT YOU WELL ENOUGH. I'VE GOT TO KNOW THIS WATER CASTE MERCHANT CALLED POR'UI [+ + DIALOGUS NOTE LIT: WATER/ENVOY, A TAU RANK EQUIVALENT + +], WHO'S BIG ON DRINKING AND GOSSIP, AND WHENEVER I VISIT TAU'N WE GET TOGETHER TO TRADE AND TALK. I TALKED TO HIM ABOUT THE RUMOURS OF TAU MERCENARIES ONE TIME AND HE SHUT RIGHT UP, WOULDN'T SAY A THING ABOUT IT. ANOTHER TIME, MONTHS LATER, HE WAS DEEP IN HIS CUPS AND HE BROUGHT IT UP HIMSELF — I RECKON HE WAS FEELING GUILTY FOR NOT SAYING ANYTHING FIRST TIME. WELL, HE SAID AS HOW IT WAS A BAD BUSINESS, TO HEAR OF TAU FIGHTING FOR PAY AND NOT THE GREATER GOOD, WHICH IS WHAT THEY OFTEN CALL THEIR EMPIRE, AND THAT THE AUN [+ + DIALOGUS NOTE: ETHEREAL CASTE + +] SHOULD DO SOMETHING ABOUT IT. HE LOOKED GUILTY FOR SAYING THAT TOO, BUT THE SPIRIT WAS IN HIM, IF YOU TAKE MY MEANING, AND HE CARRIED ON AND TOLD ME ABOUT COMMANDER FARSIGHT. SEEMS THAT FARSIGHT WAS A BIG HERO TO THE TAU, FOUGHT OFF TWO BIG ORK INVASIONS AND HELPED FIGHT AGAINST THE IMPERIAL CRUSADE TWO CENTURIES BACK. WHEN THE CRUSADE WAS OVER, FARSIGHT TOOK AN EXPEDITION OUT TO THE EDGE OF THE EMPIRE TO RECOLONISE SOME LOST OUTPOSTS, ONE OF THEM AT WHAT HE CALLED AN 'ARTEFACT WORLD' AT THE EDGE OF DAMOCLES GULF. SOMETHING HAPPENED WHEN THE EXPEDITION WAS THERE, APPARENTLY A MESSAGE-BOAT CAME BACK SAYING THERE WAS FIGHTING BUT IT SEEMED CONFUSED ABOUT WHO THE ENEMY WAS. WORSE STILL, THE AUN WITH THE EXPEDITION HAD BEEN KILLED, BUT THERE WAS NO WORD OF BY WHAT. AFTER THAT FARSIGHT HAD APPARENTLY GONE ON TO FIGHT OFF ANOTHER ORK INVASION THREATENING THE EMPIRE BUT HE NEVER CAME BACK, AND THERE WAS NO MORE WORD OF WHAT HAD BECOME OF THE EXPEDITION. POR'UI SAID THE RUMOURS MUST MEAN THAT FARSIGHT'S PEOPLE HAD SET UP COLONIES OUT IN THE GULF, IN AN AREA THE AUN NORMALLY FORBADE THE TAU SHIPS TO ENTER. HE RECKONED THAT WITHOUT THE GUIDANCE OF THE AUN THEY WERE IN DANGER OF REGRESSING TO BARBARISM, 'THE TERROR' HE CALLED IT, LIKE BEFORE THE AUN CAME, WHEN EACH CASTE WAS SET AGAINST THE OTHERS AND WOULD FIGHT TO DOMINATE EACH OTHER INSTEAD OF SIMPLY WORKING TOGETHER FOR THE GREATER GOOD. I SAID THAT IN A SET-UP LIKE THAT I COULDN'T SEE AS HOW IT COULD BE ANYTHING OTHER THAN FIRE CASTE IN CHARGE, AND HE SAID IF FARSIGHT HAD WANTED IT THAT WAY HE WOULD HAVE MADE IT LIKE THAT. WELL, POR'UI SEEMED REALLY UPSET AT THE IDEA OF THE FIRE WARRIORS RUNNING THE SHOW, AND KEPT SAYING AS HOW THEY'D WANT NOTHING BUT WAR ALL THE TIME. NOW I'VE SEEN ENOUGH FIRE WARRIORS AND TAU SHIPS TO KNOW THAT'D BE BAD FOR EVERYONE. I KNOW YOU'VE GOT THE EAR OF THE IMPERIALS, OSSNEOUS, AND I THINK YOU'D BETTER LET THEM KNOW DOUBLE QUICK THAT THERE'S SOMETHING BAD BREWING IN THE DAMOCLES GULF."

+ + + + VOX RECORD ENDS + + + + + +

AUN'SHI

	WS	BS	S	T	W	I	A	Ld	Sv	Points
Aun'shi	5	3	3	3	3	5	4	10	4+	105

Special Character: A Tau army may include Aun'shi as a special character. If you decide to take him then he counts as one of the HQ choices for the army. He must be used exactly as described below and may not be given extra equipment from the Tau Armoury.

Equipment: Honour blade, hard-wired shield generator (4+ Invulnerable save), photon grenades and EMP grenades.

Independent Character: Aun'shi is an independent character and follows the independent character special rules in the Warhammer 40,000 rulebook.

Aun'shi is more comfortable with the company of Fire warriors than many members of the Ethereal caste and will frequently accompany a squad into battle as Shas'aun'shi. He may select any Fire Warrior team and nominate it as his retinue. Such a team is clearly marked for glory.

If this option is taken, he loses his independent character privileges and becomes part of the unit. While one member of the unit remains in addition to Aun'shi, it will never count as being below half strength for purposes of holding table quarters, taking objectives or victory points.

SPECIAL RULES

Blade Master: Aun'shi is a dedicated student of the fighting arts and has been for virtually all his life. He has a level of expertise with the honour blade that few Tau can match.

• Aun'shi may use none, some or all of his Attacks to parry. He must declare how many Attacks he is using to parry at the start of close combat before any to hit dice have been rolled. For each Attack that Aun'shi gives up, reduce the number of Attacks of any enemy attacking him by one. Opponents will always get a minimum of one Attack. If, for example, he gives up two Attacks then each enemy who attacks him gets two less Attacks, but each will always get at least one.

• Aun'shi's skill is such that he can always find an opponent's weakness. He gets the usual +2 Strength bonus using the honour blade and additionally will wound any opponent if he rolls 6 to hit, with no Armour saving throw possible.

Inspiring Presence: Aun'shi's record of victory makes him loved as well as respected by the Fire caste. No Tau leader evokes the same courage and determination in his followers.

• Tau units (not Kroot or Drones) may re-roll any Morale tests if Aun'shi is on the table. This includes passed Morale tests. The re-rolled result stands. Any Tau units joined by Aun'shi become Fearless, and automatically pass all Morale checks and Pinning tests.

• Additionally, a Tau unit (not Kroot or Drones) that has been joined by Aun'shi will hurl themselves at the enemy with total confidence that they will be victorious. In close combat they will have +1 Initiative and +1 Attack while Aun'shi is with them.

Price of Failure: If Aun'shi is killed, every friendly unit of Tau on the tabletop (not Kroot or Drones) must take a Morale check at the start of their next turn if not in close combat or already falling back. Any units that fail must Fall Back in their next Movement phase.

A modest hero of many battles, Aun'shi longs for peace but is bound by duty to his comrades to wage war. Lionised by the Fire caste, he is seen as a good luck charm by those who have served with him.

"I have taken great pains not to laugh at the actions of aliens, nor to weep at them or to hate them, but to understand them."

ATTR. AUN'SHI

THE DEFENCE OF FIO'VASH

At the time of this famous battle, Aun'shi was already nearing forty years of age, old for a Tau, and was looking forward to spending his last years on the paradise sept of Au'taal. A much respected life was behind him, many long years spent helping to expand the empire into space by providing guidance for the Tau in his care. Hailing from the hot-blooded sept of Vior'la, Aun'shi had perhaps a better understanding of the Fire caste and their way of war. It is said that on occasion he even went as far as to join them in their battle rituals, honing his skills with the honour blade to a level where even the Shas'vre could not pierce his defences. His skill with a blade had reached the level where spirit, weapon and body had achieved complete harmony.

In what was supposed to be his last assignment, Aun'shi led a Tau colony force to a world he named Kel'tyr, the newest world in the expanding Tau empire. Infested by feral Orks, initial progress in claiming the world was slow but, under Aun'shi's guidance, Fire warrior teams were soon able to push the Orks back from the main areas of Tau settlements. Within four years, the world was flourishing, the Fio building many fine towns across the main continental mass. Fio'vash was one such town, a mining outpost in the low foothills of a mineral rich mountain range some four hundred miles to the east of the capital. While on a tour of inspection of the outlying towns, Aun'shi and his bodyguard became trapped in Fio'vash when a horde of feral Orks surrounded the town and launched a surprise attack to capture the mine workings.

The existing garrison of Fio'vash had been augmented by Aun'shi's Fire warrior bodyguard and the Orks were cut down in their hundreds. Early in the fighting, the Shas'vre of the Fire warriors was beheaded, cut down by an enormous Ork Nob. The loss of this heroic warrior sent a surge of panic through the ranks of the Tau warriors and it seemed as though their defence would crumble. Aun'shi leapt in front of the Nob and cut him in two with one blow from his honour blade, planting the haft of his weapon between the shorn halves of the corpse. Heartened by the Ethereal's brave defiance, the Fire warriors line steadied and they threw the Orks back. Again and again the Orks attacked Fio'vash, and each time Aun'shi led the defenders in battle, fighting alongside his warriors and spurring them to unheard of feats of valour. He despatched Stealth armoured warriors and a member of the Kor to take word to the capital, as he knew that, against so many Orks, it was only a matter of time until they were overrun.

The battle raged on, the Tau defenders silhouetted by the flames of burning buildings. The Fire warriors were fighting at the limits of courage and endurance, held together by the indomitable will of Aun'shi. Every time their line bent back under the Ork assault, Aun'shi was there, his flashing honour blade a shimmering blur of silver steel as he cut down Orks by the dozen. Aun'shi moved like quicksilver, dodging killing blows, twisting and weaving through the air in a graceful ballet of death. Wherever he struck, Orks died and soon none would go near him, so fearful were they of this warrior who could not be killed. Eventually the Tau were forced to pull back to an inner perimeter of defensive walls which the Fio had constructed, and there they prepared for the next assault. Aun'shi stood in the ranks with the surviving Fire warriors, hoping that the Kor had managed to carry word of their situation to the capital.

The Greenskins attacked again and, though the Fire warriors slew scores of Orks with every volley, they simply could not kill enough to prevent them from reaching the walls. All through the burning heat of the day, Orks charged the defensive walls, the mound of dead before it growing every second as the Fire warriors killed with grim efficiency. The walls were beginning to give in places and Orks poured through these gaps whenever they appeared, swamping Tau battlesuits and dragging them to the ground. Each time the Orks formed a wedge within a breach, Aun'shi led a counter-

attack to hurl them from the compound. As dusk approached, less than fifty Fire warriors remained alive and both forces sensed that the end was near. As the Orks massed for the final attack, Aun'shi ordered a retreat into the barricaded shrine at the town's centre, knowing that there were too few of them to hold the full length of the wall. The Fire Warriors readied their last clips of ammunition while the workers of the Fio caste took up their picks and shovels, ready to fight in hand-to-hand combat.

With a roar of pure hatred, the Orks swarmed over the wall and into the compound, burning and destroying everything in their path. Fire warriors shot from prepared loopholes, thinning the first wave of Orks, but unable to prevent it from reaching the building. Orks set about the door to the shrine with giant axes, climbing the walls to smash through the roof and screaming their bestial war-cries. The first Orks to enter the shrine were killed swiftly, but there were always more pushing their way inside. Aun'shi fought at the shrine doors as they were finally ripped from the frame. Together with the last of his Fire warriors, Aun'shi stood ready to fight, his honour blade cleaving the air before him in long, sweeping slashes. If they were to die, then they would die together.

Suddenly the Orks were thrown into silhouette as a series of rippling detonations exploded behind them. Sweeping through the flames came the bulky forms of dozens of Devilfish troop carriers, guns chattering with deadly firepower as team after team of Fire warriors poured from their interiors. Alerted by the Kor, the full wrath of the Tau now fell upon the Ork rear. Lumbering Broadside battlesuits sprayed the Orks with plasma fire, cutting them down in droves as Hammerhead tanks blasted huge holes in the Ork mobs. Within the hour, the Orks were either dead or fleeing and the leader of the recently arrived Fire warriors cadres found Aun'shi still standing at the shrine doors, his honour blade slick with Ork blood, a handful of his bodyguard left alive. Despite the terrible casualties, the defence of Fio'vash was hailed as a great victory, the Ethereal shrine still stood and the mine workings were still in Tau hands. The survivors of the siege hailed Aun'shi as a hero, the Fire warriors pledging to serve him for the rest of their lives.

News of the victory soon reached the Ethereals on T'au and, rather than allow Aun'shi to spend his remaining years on Au'taal, it was decreed that he lead fresh expeditions to expand the Tau empire. There would be no peaceful retirement for Aun'shi.

Adept Raphael Palmatus stepped off the crew ramp of his shuttle and squinted in the harsh glare of evening sunlight. The air was hot and stagnant, not a breath of wind stirred and he could feel sweat prickling on his brow. A shadow fell across him as the giant figure of Captain Taelos of the Imperial Fists joined him on the landing platform. The Space Marine seemed untroubled by the heat, despite the heavy armour and ceremonial fur cape he wore. Their shuttle sat atop an immensely tall structure and Palmatus could see for miles in all directions across the Tau city. Unlike most Imperial cities, this was elegant and very open. Gleaming towers of marble, white steel and glass soared majestically, interconnected by airy walkways and translucent bridges that seemed to defy the natural laws of gravity. He could see dozens of long rail-bound grav-trains snaking their way soundlessly through the city, crossing and intersecting in a graceful ballet, stopping briefly every now and then at various structures before moving off again.

A section of wall across the platform irised open, a robed figure emerging into the sunlight to meet them. Palmatus kept his face expressionless as he saw that the figure was not Tau, but Human. The man was powerfully built, though nowhere near as formidable as Taelos. His skin was deeply tanned and lined, the texture of old leather and his eyes sparkled with wry amusement. He raised a hand in greeting and Palmatus could see the outline of a faded Imperial Eagle tattooed on his forearm.

"Greetings. My name is Harmon Delphi and I welcome you to T'olku," said the man. Palmatus bowed in response, concealing his displeasure at this calculated insult. The tattoo on Delphi's arm marked him as a soldier of the Emperor's army and, in Imperial eyes, a deserter and traitor. He was sure that Taelos had seen it too, but thankfully the captain said nothing.

"I thank you for your greeting," he replied, "It is pleasing for us to be here and I look forward to conducting my discussions with Aun'O T'olku K'yna. I am sure that between us, he and I can resolve the Nimbosa colony dispute amicably."

"Yes..." began Delphi, spreading his hands in a gesture of apology. "Regrettably, O'K'yna has asked me to convey his most sincere apologies to you as he is extremely busy at this time and is unable to receive you at present. He hopes you'll bear with him in this, and meanwhile offers you the hospitality of the city."

Palmatus nodded politely, a measure of his earlier optimism returning. Aun'O T'olku K'yna was a fool to play these petty games. Every day they spent here in negotiations brought the retribution of the Imperial Navy closer to Nimbosa. He said graciously, "Aun'O T'olku K'yna is most considerate. Please convey to him our thanks for his hospitality as I am sure we shall enjoy our stay here. Now, if you would be so kind, please convey us to our quarters."

Delphi smiled and led them through the opening he had emerged from and along a series of featureless white corridors. Within moments, Palmatus had lost all sense of direction, though he knew they were descending into the heart of the tower. Their quarters were simple and functional, with everything they would require to satisfy their basic needs, but little else. Delphi left, explaining that the Tau stationed outside their quarters would be their guide for the duration of their stay. Palmatus knew that 'guide' really meant 'guard', and that they would see only what Aun'O T'olku K'yna wished them to.

The following morning Palmatus rose early and, along with Taelos and the Tau escort, began the exploration of the city. Taelos was like a caged Catachan Devil, unable to mask his impatience despite Palmatus' remonstrations. He wished the Space Marine captain would cease his impolite display, but knew better than to openly manifest his displeasure. He was aware that they must be under surveillance and it would not do to show division or disagreement. As the sun rose, bright and glaring, he was glad of the dermal protection unguents he had applied. Boarding one of the silver grav-trains he had seen yesterday, they were carried smoothly along the powered rail into the air, the ground many thousands of feet below. The buildings which Palmatus saw were constructed from a variety of smooth materials, seamless white stone panels, gleaming metal columns, gracefully curved glass sheets and transparent light blocks. Each was sparingly detailed and occasionally adorned with Tau symbology which the Xenolexicon servitors were even now trying to decipher. There was an elegant simplicity to the architectural style; no single building attempted to outdo another in its splendour and each was designed to fit stylistically with its neighbour.

The grav-train gradually began to descend, looping downwards through the lower levels of the city. Here the buildings were plainer, more simply designed and smaller than those in the centre of the city. Glittering arcades and geodesic domes passed by, the Tau inhabitants becoming more distinct as their journey took them towards a vast, silver sheathed dome at the edge of the city.

"Where are we going?" Palmatus asked the accompanying Tau guide.

The Tau turned his featureless helmet towards Palmatus and pointed to the huge structure ahead, "The Battle Dome, to see the warriors of the Fire Caste training. It should be quite interesting, especially for you Captain Taelos."

The Space Marine grunted and nodded, "It is always good to know how the enemy fights."

"We are not your enemy, Captain," replied the Tau, "And when you see our Fire warriors you will not desire us for one."

"I am a soldier," snapped Taelos, "I fight where my Emperor demands and if it is his will that we be enemies, then it shall be so. Desire does not enter into it."

"What I am sure the captain means," said Palmatus hurriedly, "is that a man seldom desires enemies, but ultimately has little control over his destiny. It is our fervent wish that we do not become enemies."

The alien seemed to accept this and turned away as the grav-train passed through an opening in the skin of the Battle Dome.

The sheer scale of the dome's interior took Palmatus' breath away. The ceiling swept high above them, held aloft by unknown means as there were no supporting columns visible. What little he understood regarding construction told Palmatus that such a huge structure should not be able to stand. The dome was split into arenas of various sizes, each modelled to represent a different theatre of war. There were jungle arenas, urban arenas, desert arenas, water filled arenas and all manner of others spread throughout the dome's floor. The grav-train slid to a halt over a large arena filled with prefabricated buildings, mining equipment and several armoured vehicles. The analogy was not lost on Palmatus. This was a small-scale recreation of the Nimbosa colony and, while the mocked-up vehicles were crude, the resemblance to Imperial patterns was unmistakable.

Advancing through the colony were several bulky figures; Fire warriors armoured in heavy battlesuits. Each warrior carried a fearsome looking weapon and was also armed with a second, shoulder-mounted gun. Before them, two squads of lighter armoured Fire warriors darted through the colony, firing from cover in support of one another. One of the mock-ups of an Imperial tank rumbled forwards, weapons firing and forcing the troops in the vanguard into cover. As one, the weapons of the heavy battlesuits locked onto the tank and fired, blowing it apart in a spectacular explosion and blasting the turret high into the air. The mock colony was swiftly taken and the grav-train moved off again.

For the next two hours, Palmatus and Taelos were shown Tau Fire warriors training in a variety of different warzones and employing all manner of exotic weaponry, vehicles and wargear. By the time they emerged once more into the daylight, Palmatus could see that Taelos had a new found respect for the Tau way of war.

As the grav-train began climbing high into the centre of the city once again, the Tau guide removed his helmet and laid it beside him. His face bore the same typically flat features of the Tau, but in the centre of his forehead was a diamond shaped ridge of raised bone. Lustrous dark hair spilled from the top of his head in an elaborately jewelled scalp lock and his narrow eyes were twin slits of black.

The alien fixed his gaze on Palmatus and said, "You have seen what my warriors can do, Raphael. Can you not see the foolishness of your continued resistance to our colonists on Nimbosa? I respect your people, they are brave and have done all that honour demands, but they cannot stand against us. You came here to begin protracted negotiations in order to delay our attack and allow your own forces time to reach Nimbosa. That will not happen. The Kor bring me word that your vessels are many months away and Nimbosa will be ours long before that."

Captain Taelos began to speak, but Palmatus smoothly interrupted, saying, "I presume then that you are Aun'O T'olku K'yna."

"I have that honour, yes," nodded the Tau Ethereal.

"Then you should know that when our ships arrive at Nimbosa we will fight you. The Emperor does not give up worlds His servants have claimed in His name."

"You are a wise man, Raphael Palmatus, and, despite his modest words, I know that your military advisor here is no ordinary soldier. You should both go back to your Emperor and tell him what you have seen here. Tell him of all the people that will die in his name and ask him if it is worth such a price to stand in our way."

"We will fight you, alien," snarled Captain Taelos, "To the last drop of blood we will fight you."

"I know," replied the Tau sadly and turned away.

THOUGHTS ON TAU LANGUAGE

Sister Verity, Order Dialogus

At the request of Explorator Magos Dana Aquila I began studies on the language and dialect of the race known as Tau. It is a complex, highly evolved form of communication and, even after six months of intensive study (with the aid of a team of Xenolexicon Servitors), I have only begun to scratch the surface of this fluid language. In sound it is deeply lyrical and soft, with many words and meanings dependant on intonation, glottal emphasis and even posture. The underlying structure of the language alone took the servitors some two months to break down into recognisable High Gothic. Added to this, its multiple arrangements of polysyllabic word groups renders it difficult in the extreme for human vocal cords to pronounce. It will take a skilful linguist indeed to speak even the most basic Tau words and phrases. I would respectfully suggest that my studies into this alien language would render my humble self an ideal candidate for further contact with this highly developed race.

The Tau have many ways of referring to one another and their names are worthy of many months of specific study alone. To the Tau, the most important part of their name is the caste they are born into and this forms the first portion of their identity. Broadly speaking, the Tau are organised into four main castes that correspond to the four elements, fire (Shas), earth (Fio), air (Kor) and water (Por). Each caste fulfils a distinct role within the Tau civilisation and seems to hark back to the evolutionary development of the race.

The Fire caste are the soldiers of the Tau and I was fortunate enough to see some of these fearsome warriors training in their armoured battlesuits (cross ref file: T232/U3: Tau way of war). The labourers, builders and artisans are those Tau of the earth caste. They are the sustaining caste without whom Tau society could not

function. (Ordo Xenos note: Investigations into effects of this caste being exterminated should be undertaken.) Although I saw almost none of the air caste during my stay here, I understand them to be messengers and the pilots of Tau ships. I believe most of the air caste remain in space as it would be hazardous in the extreme for them to return to a natural gravity environment. Lastly, the water caste, of whom I was to have the most contact with, are the diplomats and

administrators, those who facilitate the smooth workings of the other castes. I was also able to collate scattered hints of a fifth caste, whose name (Aun) can be variously translated as 'Celestial' or 'Ethereal', but the Tau assigned to me steadfastly refused to be drawn on the subject. I shall forward further information on this caste as I obtain it.

With the caste of a Tau established, the second portion of their name appears to refer to their rank within society. The Tau are perhaps unique in all the species I have encountered in that there is no stigma attached to any rank or profession. Each Tau has his or her place in society and enjoys the respect of their peers no matter how menial a task they perform. Each role is recognised as being part of the greater whole and a furtherance of the common good. There appears to be five major levels of Tau rank, each of which has a subtly different meaning dependent on the caste to which it is suffixed. In ascending order of seniority these ranks are as follows (I have included the best Imperial equivalent of each rank based upon the nuances of the fire caste):

'La - warrior

'Ui - veteran

'Vre - hero

'El - noble (or possibly knight)

'O - commander

Next in a Tau's name comes his 'Sept' which translates as either his extended family or place of birth. This portion of the Tau name is open to the widest interpretations and has many subtle differences in meaning. For example, a

Tau from one of the elder worlds (Septs) may be perceived as wiser or more sophisticated by implication than one from a younger Sept who in turn are regarded as more dynamic and practical. Certain worlds also contain meaning in themselves and can embody a particular trait within the Tau who originate from these worlds. For example, the name of the Tau planet of Vior'la means 'hot blooded' and is known as a particularly aggressive fire caste world. Other such planets include Bork'an, which is regarded as a centre of learning and study. I have yet to plumb the full implications of the Septs and their overall relation to Tau society but shall assuredly continue to do so.

Lastly comes a Tau's individual name and it appears that these names are earned in recognition of some achievement rather than given at birth as is the case with humans. These are perhaps the most puzzling element of the Tau name and while some of their names may be relatively easily understood, such as 'Shovah' (far-sighted) or 'Kais' (skilful) others are more perplexing. What might a Tau known as 'Vral' (undercut) or

'Tsua'm' (middle) have accomplished to earn such a name? It is also possible for some remarkable individuals to accumulate more than one name in his lifetime. Some of the more notable Tau I was introduced to had literally dozens of names. I have since learned that it is common for these Tau to truncate their full names and be known by a much simplified appellation. As an example of how the Tau titles translate, the name Shas'O Vior'la Shovah Kais Mont'yr can be broken down as follows. This individual is a member of the fire caste (Shas), holds the rank of commander ('O), hails from the world of Vior'la and has the personal names that translate as farsighted (Shovah), skilful (Kais) and blooded (Mont'yr). However, this Tau is more commonly known as O'Shovah or Commander Farsight and this form of address is much more popular with Tau of great accomplishment.

How the Tau refer to and address one another adds yet another layer of complexity to their relationships and language. For example, referring to a

Tau by his individual name is regarded as overly familiar unless the Tau is part of a 'Ta'lissera' (see later). It is considered polite to refer to a Tau by their caste name and rank as this acknowledges his or her place in society. As noted earlier, there is no shame in performing menial tasks and, by referring to a Tau's role as a form of address, that task is recognised and respected. Each individual is seen as contributing to the advance of the race and is therefore worthy of respect.

Another term that came up in relation to Tau forms of address is 'Ta'lissera'. The best translation which the Xenolexicons could derive for this word was communion or marriage. It appears to be some kind of sworn bond where groups of Tau pledge support and community to one another. The Tau who have sworn these pledges may address each other by their individual names and are much admired. This bond is seen as the ultimate Tau expression of respect for one another as it symbolises the sacrifice of individual pride to become part of a greater whole. The 'Ta'lissera' is most commonly found within the ranks of Fire caste warriors and Earth caste work teams and, I must confess, it seems to be a noble and worthy concept. (Ordo Xenos addendum: It is recommended that Sister Verity be questioned regarding possible alien contamination.)

Attached to this report is the nearest approximation which the Xenolexicon Servitors could devise in regards to a Tau alphabet and a brief lexicon of common Tau words.

TAU WORD	BEST TRANSLATION
Aun	Ethereal
Aun'bork'an'retha	A combined temple/university on Bork'an dedicated to the Ethereal Caste & their wisdom.
El	Second highest Tau rank. Fire: Noble or Knight; Air: Captain; Earth: Engineer; Water: Diplomat; Ethereal: Holy?
Fio	Earth
Gue'la	Tau word for humans
J'kaara	Mirror
Kais	Skilful
Kauyon	Patient / Hunter
Ko'vash	To strive for (Lit. A Worthy Cause)
Kor	Air
Kor'vesa	Tau drone (Lit. Faithful helper)
La	Lowest Tau rank. Fire: Warrior; Air: Messenger; Earth: Worker; Water: Bureaucrat; Ethereal: Prince
M'yen	Unforseen
Mal'caor	Spider
Mesme	Combination
Mont'au	The Terror. The Tau race's worst nightmare. The time before the coming of the Ethereal caste when the other castes were set against one another. A barbaric time of war that the Tau fear could return should any Tau put themselves before the Greater Good.
Mont'ka	Killing Blow
Mont'yr	Blooded (Lit. Seen battle)
O	Highest Tau rank. Fire: Commander; Air: Admiral; Earth: Planner; Water: Ambassador; Ethereal: Highest(?)

TAU WORD	BEST TRANSLATION
Or'es	Powerful
Por	Water
Run'al	A small observation post or hide
Shas	Fire
Shas'ar'tol	Fire caste military high command
Shi	Victory
Shovah	Farsighted
Ta'lissera	Communion/Marriage. Refers to a bonding ritual where groups of Tau, commonly Fire Warriors or Earth caste work teams, swear bonds of loyalty and support to one another. Much respected by other Tau as it represents an individual giving up his own desires for the greater good of the empire.
Tau'va	The Greater Good, something the Tau are taught from an early age to strive for.
Tsua'm	Middle
Ui	Second lowest Tau rank. Fire: Veteran; Air: Carrier; Earth: Senior; Water: Envoy; Ethereal: Prelate
Ukos	Spoon
Vash'ya	Between Spheres
Vior'la	Hot Blooded
Vral	Undercut
Vre	Middle Tau rank. Fire: Hero; Air: Pilot; Earth: Overseer; Water: Magister; Ethereal: King
Y'eldi	Air cast name for a particularly gifted pilot (Lit. Winged One)

THE TAU ALPHABET

⊐	A	◻	G	◻	P
◻	B	⊍	H	⊟	R
◻	C/K	⅂	I/Y	⊟	S
⊐	D	⊒	J	T	T
⊓	E	⅃	L	⊍	U
⊍	F	⊓	M	⊌	V
		⊓	N	◻	W
		⊏	O	♩	X

ASIDE ON TAU TIME KEEPING

The Tau'cyr is an annual cycle on Tau.

A Tau'cyr is broken down into 6 Kai'rotaa each of 80 rotaa, each Kai'rotaa is dedicated to a caste with the additional one dedicated to the race as a whole.

A rotaa is broken down into ten decs, decs are either light-time or dark-time. Most Tau need only 1-2 decs of sleep per rotaa.

Conversion

The Tau'cyr or Tau year lasts approximately 300 Terran days (297.74 to be precise). A Kai'rotaa is therefore about 50 Terran days. A rotaa is approximately 15 Terran hours and a dec is 1.5 Terran hours.

THE DAMOCLES GULF CRUSADE

The Damocles Crusade was a military action typical of the Eastern Fringe before the arrival of the Tyranid Hive Fleets. Wherever possible, when challenges to the Imperium were discovered, war followed. In 742.M41 another such Crusade was to be unleashed in the Lithesh Sector. A string of Imperial sub-sectors stretching out between the Damocles Gulf and the Perdus Rift Anomaly had suffered extensive disruption due to Eldar pirate raids and warp storm activity. As the Imperium strove to restore its grip in the region, it was discovered that an alien race called the Tau were allying themselves with dissident Imperial factions. The peril of these local alliances was evident in the number of alien goods and artefacts appearing in nearby systems.

Inquisitorial investigation revealed evidence of Tau activity in adjoining sectors. The conclusion was that they represented a major threat, and Cardinal Esau Gurney of Brimlock officially called for a crusade to be dispatched to purge the aliens.

The crusade was based around a dozen capital ships, five provisional companies of Space Marines made up of contingents from a dozen Chapters, and nineteen regiments of Imperial Guard, seven of them from Brimlock. The first move was towards the Timbra sub-sector where human colonists had co-existed with the aliens. The Crusade first reasserted Imperial rule in the Garrus and Kleist colonies. Individuals implicated in dealing with the Tau were seized and punished at a special assize held before the furious crusaders. The Imperial colonies secured, the crusade moved on and engaged the Tau for the first time in the uninhabited Hydass system.

FIRST CONTACT: FLEET ACTION IN THE HYDASS SYSTEM.

Seven Tau warships of approximately cruiser displacement were detected on the edge of the system. The crusade fleet attacked immediately, but found the Tau ships to be capable of launching powerful torpedo salvos at long range, breaking up the Imperial formation. Bomber waves were launched but these were countered by Tau escorts launched from the capital ships. A Space Marine strike cruiser supported by a squadron of Sword class frigates made the decisive attack. Getting inside the Tau formation, they inflicted heavy damage and discovered that Tau ships lacked broadside firepower. The Tau launched more escorts as a screen while they disengaged. One Tau ship was unable to withdraw and exploded while the crew was in the process of abandoning their craft.

GROUND WAR
THE LANDING ON SY'L'KELL.

The Sy'l'kell system contained an apparently fertile agri-world with a population estimated at seven million Tau. It was defended by an orbital station, a number of system ships and the remnants of the Tau fleet encountered at Hydass. The crusader council of war appointed Captain Rumann of the Iron Hands to take overall command of the planetary assault. The Imperial fleet closed quickly, pounding the orbital station as they approached. Its armaments were not as extensive as had been feared, though, and the Iron Hands boarded it. The Tau fleet disengaged almost immediately and was not seriously damaged. It was conjectured that they were evacuating key personnel from the planet rather than defending it. The Iron Hands quickly overwhelmed the orbital station's defenders and dutifully cleansed it with flame. It was to serve as Imperial headquarters for the ground campaign.

Space Marines from the Scythes of the Emperor established a landing zone and the 17th Brimlock Dragoons were landed to provide heavy support. The Tau response was swift and consisted of an extremely well-equipped mechanised infantry formation with armoured support. The Tau grav-tank, designated as the Hammerhead, appeared to be a close match for the Leman Russ, and the Tau proved most adept at supporting their armour with infantry. The Dragoons suffered heavy losses when enemy infantry wearing heavy jump armour ambushed them in rolling ground. Only swift intervention from the 4th Stormtrooper Company and the Scythes of the Emperor averted a massacre.

While the crusade pushed ever nearer Sy'l'kell's population centres, the Tau evacuated the most qualified workers and dismantled any advanced technology. When the 9th Brimlock Fusiliers were landed, the Tau resistance crumbled and all objectives were quickly attained. The planet was duly cleansed.

THE PURGING OF VISS'EL

While arrangements were made to cross the Damocles Gulf to the Imperial designated sub-sector of Kendral, an expeditionary force was sent to deal with the Tau presence in the Viss'el system. Early reconnaissance had revealed the sixth planet to be an ice covered water world on which the Tau had established fishery colonies. As no great strategic benefit was evident to controlling the planet, it was subjected to orbital bombardment, melting the ice around the main colonies and destroying them.

THE DAL'YTH CAMPAIGN

STAGE 1:
NEAR DISASTER AT PRA'YEN.

After a five month journey across the Gulf, the Crusade arrived in the Dal'yth system within the Kendral sub-sector. The outermost planet, Pra'yen, was protected by an orbital station and was clearly intended to provide the first line of a system defence. The fleet approach was too casual, assuming the station to be no more dangerous than that already encountered. It proved to be much more formidable, mounting an array of heavy railguns whose first volley crippled the *Honour of Damlass*. The fleet broke formation just as eleven Tau ships emerged from behind Pra'yen. The fleet escorts attacked the orbital station while the main battlefleet swung towards the Tau ships. The Tau fleet concentrated its torpedo salvos against the *Regent Lakshimbai*, a Dauntless class light cruiser, which resisted superbly until a lucky shot caused massive bulkhead collapse which in turn triggered a plasma drive overload, destroying the ship with all hands. Arriving piecemeal, the Imperial ships gradually won the advantage, although on this occasion the Tau fought on despite taking horrendous punishment.

The escorts suffered heavy losses fighting the Tau orbital station. As soon as they were closely engaged, though, the last piece of the Tau trap was put into place. Appearing from nowhere after suddenly powering up, a Kroot warsphere steered directly for the Imperial transports. The transport flotilla had no choice but to scatter. Fortunately the huge Kroot hulk was slow and its guns short-ranged, but its sheer size seemed certain to eradicate the crusade.

Salvation came in the form of Admiral Jallaque's flagship, the *Blade of Woe*, a Retribution class battleship. Leaving the rest of the fleet to finish off the Tau warships, the Admiral had turned about, planning to help the escorts when the warsphere arrived. Accelerating to maximum power, the great ship overtook the lumbering warsphere and turned across its path. From the first exchange it was clear that the *Blade of Woe* carried the greater weight of fire and its salvos systematically ripped the warsphere apart.

The crusading fleet had won a truly pyrrhic victory. Although the warsphere, Tau fleet and orbital station were destroyed, it was at a cost of four capital ships and fourteen escorts. The Tau ambush had come very close to succeeding and brought a new respect for the Tau to the Imperial fleet.

STAGE 2: STALEMATE AT DAL'YTH PRIME

Although some amongst the crusade's command advocated turning back, the lure of a major Tau world lying ahead was too tempting. Dal'yth Prime was protected by three orbital stations and, after recent experience, these were approached very cautiously. None proved to be heavily gunned though, and were destroyed at leisure.

Expecting a new Tau fleet at any time, the ground assault quickly commenced. The eastern seaboard of the largest continent was selected as the target. Protected to the north by mountains and to the east by the sea, a short advance south-west put the invasion force before the first of a number of cities forming a conurbation along the coast.

The drop was contested by large numbers of Tau flyers but was eventually successful. The full force of the crusade was finally deployed and the invasion began. The local road network was excellent and the advance neared the Tau city of Gel'bryn before a defensive line was formed.

With Titans and armoured formations as the spearhead, the crusade ploughed relentlessly toward the city. As they advanced though, enemy missiles, fired from beyond hills and woods, started to inflict heavy losses. Units had to be detached to drive back the Tau spotters, but these were in turn engaged by Tau jump troops equipped with cloaking fields. Gradually the coherency of the attacking wedge was broken up until, by the time it reached the outskirts of Gel'bryn, there were three spearheads pushing forward ahead of the main force. One of these was made up of Titans from the Legio Thanataris. This was countered by Tau Manta Missile Destroyers, the same craft that had been launched in the earlier space battles from the Tau warships. The second spearhead was predominantly veteran light infantry of the Rakarshan Rifles, whose intelligent use of cover had thus far kept them out of harm's way. They were countered by the emergence of a host of Kroot warriors on the rooftops and within the buildings of Gel'bryn. The third was a detachment of crusading Space Marines consisting of brethren from the Iron Hands, the Ultramarines and the Scythes of the Emperor. These the Tau countered with their own finest – their heavy jump troops. The timely Tau counter-attacks stalled the momentum of the Imperial advance and the front stabilised on the line of a broad river some twenty miles north of Gel'bryn.

STAGE 3: OPERATION HYDRA

Their advance halted, the Imperial forces, commanded in this operation by General Wendall Gauge, had to dig in to avoid the worst of the Tau firepower. The Tau possessed superior night-fighting capabilities which they exploited, moving up to extreme range and opening fire, only to withdraw at dawn. Space Marine combat patrols helped, but losses continued to mount. This was compounded by the constant worry that a new Tau fleet would arrive; the crusade fleet was badly damaged and could barely protect its transports, let alone provide cover for the army. As the siege ground on, more Tau arrived at the front each day.

General Gauge concluded that the crusade had stumbled onto a major Tau world and that his resources were insufficient for the task set them. Plentiful reinforcements had been promised at the outset but none had arrived. Inquisitor Grand was all for evacuation followed by exterminatus, as the Tau were clearly too dangerous to be allowed to exist. The army had found the Tau to be honourable adversaries, however, and there was a marked opposition to such an extreme sanction within the high command. While the crusader council of war was paralysed by internal debate, General Gauge acted. He formed the Titans up with the Brimlock regiments and attempted to force the river line down the right flank, trapping the Tau against the sea. As preparation, his artillery pounded other sectors and the Imperial Navy fighters began an offensive against Tau airfields that was costly but kept Tau flyers from the front. The Imperial strike force took their primary objective in

the first few hours – a town containing a bridge, and achieved complete surprise. As the assault continued, it was countered by ultra-mobile Tau units deployed from the ubiquitous Manta missile destroyers. For the rest of the day, a running battle was fought through the Dal'yth suburbs which ended with the Imperium a mere five miles away from trapping tens of thousands of Tau. Overnight, the Tau troops disengaged and fell back to another defensive line beyond Gel'bryn. By the morning the Tau were gone and, while the city itself was infested by lurking Kroot, the starport on the outskirts was quickly secured.

The starport, combined with the distance which the Tau had retired, made an excellent opportunity for evacuation and General Gauge took it. Resistance from the Inquisition and Adeptus Astartes was overruled by the arrival of an express order from Inquisitor Kryptman to return to Brimlock with all available forces. The Tau sensibly realised that getting in the way would serve no sane purpose and parleys held under flags of truce were honoured by both sides. The first seeds of cooperation were sown, though these would take time to bloom in the aftermath of such a brutal conflict.

The Imperium had learned to respect the Tau skills of war and the Tau had discovered the true scale and bitterness of a galaxy that they had previously thought to be theirs for the taking.

The three Fire warriors gathered in the centre of the battle dome, their Crisis battlesuits standing inert behind them. Each was stripped to the waist, bare chests slick with blood and sweat. The team leader, Vre'myar, stepped forward and drew a glittering knife from a lovingly tooled scabbard. The bonding knife had been made by Fio'vre Fal'shia Gwial specifically for the Ta'lissera ritual and was a work of art as much as a weapon. Vre'myar looked into the faces of his two fellow warriors, his new family. They had fought together for eight years and he knew the strengths and skills of both better than they did themselves. Today they had survived their second Trial by Fire and unanimously decided that the time was right to perform the bonding ritual. The air in the dome was hot following the battle drills, hundreds of the Shas gathering to witness them perform the Ta'lissera. By doing this they were sacrificing their own desires and individuality within the empire for the sake of this band of warriors, for the Greater Good. Vre'myar felt the weight of the bonding knife in his hand, very aware of the responsibility it represented. The blood of his brothers-to-be would soon coat its blade with a ruddy red sheen and the enormity of what they were about to do both thrilled and scared him.

"Come on then Vre'myar," said Ui'rash'ya, "Let us do this before we all die of old age and the Ky'husa gets cold."

"Aye," agreed Ui'lyr'sa wryly, "before the Shas'el think we have lost our nerve.'

Vre'myar smiled, raising the knife before him. He turned to his brothers and placed the tip of the blade in the centre of Ui'rash'ya's chest.

"By the power of my blood and the blood of my fellow warriors, I pledge that we shall be forever bound as brothers," said Vre'myar, repeating the Pledge of Communion. He looked Ui'rash'ya in the eyes and pressed the knife point into his skin. Blood streamed from his friend's chest, running down the blade and dripping from the elaborately carved handle. The veteran warrior did not flinch as the blade sliced downwards, carving the symbol of the Vior'la sept into the meat of his flesh. Vre'myar nodded and said, "My life is your life, your life is my life. What we do now, we do together. I have no place outside this band and all that I do from this moment is in its name." As he spoke the words, an immense contentment settled upon him and he felt fierce pride swell within his chest. Ui'rash'ya nodded in understanding, beads of sweat dripping from his forehead.

Vre'myar finished cutting and stepped back. "Not that bad was it Ui'rash'ya?"

"I have felt worse," admitted the Fire warrior placing his hand on Vre'myar's shoulder. "Well done."

Vre'myar repeated the ritual with Ui'lyr'sa and handed the blade to his friend upon its completion, eagerly awaiting his own scarring. He nodded to Ui'lyr'sa as he felt the blade pierce his skin, bunching his fists as the blade cut into him. The pain was great, but the honour of what they were doing made such concerns irrelevant. At last it was over and, breathless, Vre'myar took the bonding knife back from Ui'lyr'sa, standing before each of his fellows in turn and slashing the blade diagonally across their palms. He cleaned the blade before sheathing it in its scabbard and extended his arms. The group linked hands and, in unison, said, "Let all bear witness to this Ta'lissera. Like the eternal circle, these bonds shall never be broken. For so as long as one of us remains alive, so too do the others. There is no one Tau above another; all are as one and the whole shall be greater than the sum of its parts."

The three Fire warriors released their hold on one another's hands and knelt to pick up ceramic bowls at their feet, steam curling from the hot liquid within. Ui'rash'ya said, "Best to take Ky'husa in a single gulp," and threw the hot spirit down his throat. Vre'myar and Ui'lyr'sa gasped as the liquid fire burned its way down their gullets, a huge cheer echoing around the dome as the assembled warriors honoured them, and Vre'myar could remember no finer feeling.

"I have followed the myriad potential futures of the Tau with great interest. Though barely even striplings compared to us, I feel a strange protectiveness towards them. In time I believe they will exceed even our greatest feats and master the darkness within their souls."

ELDRAD ULTHRAN, FARSEER OF ULTHWÉ CRAFTWORLD

MISSION: HOSTAGE SITUATION

OVERVIEW

A Tau Ethereal has had to crash-land over a warzone. He is an Aun'o and cannot be allowed to be captured or killed. Fortunately, his ship was equipped with a survival pod with a powerful force field that will ensure the Aun'o's survival until its power source is exhausted. Unfortunately, it has been detected by one of the enemy forces on the planet. The Tau force must land and secure the safety of the Aun'o before the survival pod is breached.

SCENARIO SPECIAL RULES

Reserves, Deep Strike, Random Game Length, plus Night Fight on the roll of a 4+ on 1D6.

SET-UP

1. A counter or model representing the survival pod is placed in the absolute centre of the table.

2. The Tau player deploys his entire army by Deep Strike on Turn 1. Even those troops that may not Deep Strike normally can do so in this mission.

3. The non-Tau player's entire army starts in reserve and gets first turn. They enter from a single random table edge. Any units able to Deep Strike may do so.

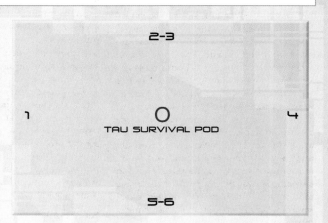

MISSION OBJECTIVE

When the random game length expires, the force field around the Tau survival pod collapses and the Ethereal is either rescued or captured.

Units greater than half strength or undamaged mobile vehicles are needed to capture the pod. Whichever side has a model or models meeting the criteria nearest to the survival pod at the end of the game wins.

RESERVES

See Set-up.
The non-Tau player starts in reserve.

GAME LENGTH

The game lasts for a random number of turns (see the Scenario special rules in the Warhammer 40,000 rulebook).

LINE OF RETREAT

Any non-Tau unit forced to fall back does so towards the table edge by which it entered the table.

Any Tau unit forced to fall back does so towards the opposite edge.

REPORT TRANSMITTED:
KORWYN DELTA

DESTINATION: MARS

DATE: 5432999.M41

TELEPATHIC DUCT:
ASTROPATH-TERMINUS TORUGAN

REF:ADMECH/99348844/XEN583

AUTHOR: GENETOR SECUNDUS ZACHARY SANTIAGO

TITLE: COGITATION ON THE EVOLUTIONARY PROCESS
AND TECHNOLOGICAL HERESY OF THE TAU RACE.

EVOLUTION

WITH INCREASED CONTACT BEING MADE WITH THE XENOS KNOWN AS TAU, IT IS BECOMING INCREASINGLY APPARENT THAT, WITH THE EXCEPTION OF TYRANIDS, THIS RACE HAS DISPLAYED A RISE TO PROMINENCE UNLIKE ANY OTHER. THE FIRST RECORDED CONTACT WITH THE TAU, SOME SIX THOUSAND YEARS AGO, FOUND THEM IN A PRIMITIVE STATE, HAVING ONLY RECENTLY MASTERED THE USE OF SIMPLE CLUBS AND FIRE. FURTHER INFORMATION IS EXTREMELY SCARCE AS THE PLANET APPEARS TO HAVE BEEN ISOLATED FOR MANY THOUSANDS OF YEARS BY WARP STORMS OF UNUSUAL FEROCITY AND DURATION. RENEWED CONTACT HAS REVEALED AN EVOLUTIONARY LEAP FAR BEYOND WHAT WOULD NORMALLY BE EXPECTED. SINCE THEY WERE FIRST CATALOGUED, THE TAU HAVE PROGRESSED TO A TECHNOLOGICAL LEVEL THAT, WHILE OBVIOUSLY NOT AS ENLIGHTENED AS THAT OF OUR OWN BLESSED ORDER, IS NEVERTHELESS HIGHLY ADVANCED. DEUS EX MECHANICUS, ALL PRAISE TO THE OMNISSIAH!

I HAVE UNDERTAKEN THIS STUDY TO DEDUCE THE ORIGIN OF THE TAU IN ORDER TO DISCOVER WHETHER THIS PROGRESSION IS THE RESULT OF NATURAL SELECTION OR SOME OTHER EXTERNAL FORCE. NATURAL SELECTION IS AN EVOLUTIONARY MECHANISM THAT TAKES PLACE WHEN SELECTED INDIVIDUALS OF A POPULATION ARE BETTER ABLE TO ADAPT TO THEIR ENVIRONMENT AND, CONSEQUENTLY, PRODUCE MORE OFFSPRING. NATURE ULTIMATELY SELECTS THOSE INDIVIDUALS WITH THE TRAITS MOST LIKELY TO SURVIVE INTO ADULTHOOD AND REPRODUCE.

AS A CONSEQUENCE, THE RESULTING EVOLUTION IS SO GRADUAL AS TO BE ALMOST IMPOSSIBLE TO DETECT IN ONLY A FEW GENERATIONS. HOWEVER, IN THE CASE OF THE TAU THERE IS EVIDENCE TO SUGGEST THAT THEIR SPECIES UNDERWENT SHORT PERIODS OF ULTRA-RAPID CHANGE. WE CAN ONLY GUESS WHAT CAUSED THESE CHANGES, PERHAPS CLIMATALOGICAL VARIANCE, ALTERED FEEDING PATTERNS OF PREDATORS, FOOD SUPPLY OR SOME UNKNOWN EXTERNAL FACTOR (SEE ATTACHED GRAPH AD/MECH32). THE RESULT WOULD BE AN ACCELERATED RATE OF CHANGE IN GENE POOL FREQUENCIES OF THE TRAITS THAT BECAME MOST FAVOURED BY THE NEW ENVIRONMENTAL CONDITIONS.

IT IS NOW QUITE APPARENT THAT THE EVOLUTIONARY HISTORY OF THE TAU IS EXTREMELY COMPLICATED. DIFFERENT SUB-SPECIES HAVE EVOLVED AT DIFFERENT RATES AND THOSE RATES HAVE CHANGED THROUGH TIME IN RESPONSE TO COMPLEX PATTERNS OF INTERACTION WITH OTHER SPECIES AND ENVIRONMENTAL FACTORS. WHAT THESE INTERACTIONS WERE WE CAN ONLY GUESS AT, GIVEN THE LITTLE INFORMATION WE WERE ABLE TO EXTRACT FROM THE TAU TEST SUBJECT ON HIS RACE'S EARLY HISTORY. FROM THE INFORMATION GLEANED, I HUMBLY ADVANCE A THEORY TO EXPLAIN THE EVOLUTION OF THE TAU WHICH I CALL 'ZACHARY'S THEOREM OF ADAPTIVE DIVERGENCE'.

DRIVEN BY NATURAL SELECTION, ADAPTIVE DIVERGENCE IS THE DIVERSIFICATION OF A SPECIES INTO TWO OR MORE SUB-SPECIES AS GROUPS ADAPT TO THEIR DISTINCT ENVIRONMENT. I BELIEVE THAT THE INITIAL STEP IS THE SEPARATION OF A SPECIES INTO DISTINCT BREEDING POPULATIONS WHICH COULD OCCUR AS A RESULT OF GEOGRAPHIC OR SOCIAL ISOLATION. OVER TIME, THE GENE POOLS OF THE ISOLATED GROUPS WOULD DIVERGE FROM EACH OTHER BY GRADUALLY ACQUIRING RANDOM MUTATIONS OR AS A RESULT OF GENETIC DRIFT. IN OTHER WORDS, NATURE SELECTS DIFFERENT TRAITS TO EXIST WITHIN THE GENE POOL OF THE DIFFERENT POPULATIONS. OVER TIME, THE POPULATIONS GENETICALLY DIVERGE ENOUGH SO THAT, TO ALL INTENTS AND PURPOSES, THEY BECOME SEPARATE SUB-SPECIES. ONE WOULD NORMALLY EXPECT THIS PROCESS TO TAKE MILLIONS OF YEARS, BUT EVIDENCE OF SYNTHETIC PROTEINS AND AMINO ACID CHAINS WITHIN THE TEST SUBJECT'S INTERNAL ORGANS LEADS ME TO BELIEVE THAT THIS PROCESS MAY HAVE BEEN ACCELERATED SOMEHOW. HOW THIS HERESY AGAINST NATURE COULD HAVE OCCURRED IS BEYOND THE SCOPE OF THIS DOCUMENT AND A MYSTERY I LEAVE TO OTHER, MORE QUALIFIED INVESTIGATORS.

TECHNOLOGY

THE HERESY OF THESE ALIENS REACHES ITS ZENITH WHEN ONE LOOKS AT THEIR TECHNOLOGY. WHILE, ADMITTEDLY, ITS PERFORMANCE CAN MATCH AND OCCASIONALLY EXCEED THAT OF IMPERIAL MANUFACTURE, IT DISPLAYS NONE OF THE PROPER OBEISANCES TO THE HOLY SPIRIT OF THE MACHINE GOD. SUCH EFFRONTERY I CAN SCARCE BELIEVE AND I RECOMMEND THAT ALL RECOVERED TAU ARTEFACTS BE DESTROYED (IN ACCORDANCE WITH ADEPTUS MECHANICUS DIRECTIVE ADMECH666). IT IS ON THE EASTERN FRONTIER THAT ONE FINDS THE MOST BLATANT DISREGARD FOR IMPERIAL DOCTRINE, WITH MANY OUTLYING COLONIES TRADING WITH THESE ALIENS FOR THEIR TECHNOLOGY IN THE FORM OF IMPROVED CONSTRUCTION AND AGRICULTURAL MACHINERY. WHERE IMPERIAL SERVANTS HAVE DISCOVERED SUCH ILLEGAL ARTEFACTS THEY HAVE SEIZED THEM AND PLACED THE OFFENDING COLONISTS IN PENAL SERVITUDE.

MORE DIFFICULT TO ENFORCE IS WHEN SUCH TECHNOLOGY FINDS ITS WAY INTO THE HANDS OF THOSE IN POSITIONS OF AUTHORITY OR ARE DIFFICULT TO TRACE. ONE EXAMPLE IS THE HUNTING RIG OF THE SO CALLED 'SPYRE HUNTER' GANGS FOUND IN THE NECROMUNDA HIVE COMPLEXES (CF: ORDO XENOS FILE 4353/ALIEN TECHNOLOGY/B). THESE ARISTOCRATIC NE'ER-DO-WELLS WEAR ARMOURED BATTLESUITS SAID TO BE SELF SUSTAINING, SELF REPAIRING AND FULLY CAPABLE OF RECORDING THE WEARER'S EVERY ACTION. THE IMPLICATIONS OF THIS LAST FACILITY ARE TRULY HORRIFYING. DOES THIS INFORMATION RETURN TO THE TAU? HAVE THESE ALIENS BEEN USING THESE TECHNOLOGICAL ABOMINATIONS TO SPY ON OUR CITIES FOR ALL THESE YEARS? IT IS IMPERATIVE THAT THESE GANGS BE MADE TO HAND OVER THEIR HUNTING RIGS LEST THE TAU GARNER EVEN MORE INFORMATION CONCERNING THE IMPERIUM.

THE INSIDIOUS INFLUENCE OF THESE ALIENS SHOULD NOT BE UNDERESTIMATED. THEIR TECHNOLOGY HAS ALREADY SPREAD TO WORLDS DEEP WITHIN THE SEGMENTUM SOLAR AND PERHAPS TO HOLY TERRA ITSELF (THOUGH SURELY NO LOYAL CITIZEN COULD POSSIBLY COUNTENANCE SUCH BLASPHEMY). THOUGH IT IS NOT WITHIN MY PURVIEW TO ADVISE ON IMPERIAL POLICY, I URGE THE RECIPIENTS OF THIS DOCUMENT TO PURSUE THE PERSECUTION OF THESE DEVIANT ALIENS WITH THE UTMOST VIGOUR WHEREVER ENCOUNTERED.

YOUR HUMBLE SERVANT,

GENETOR SECUNDUS, ZACHARY SANTIAGO

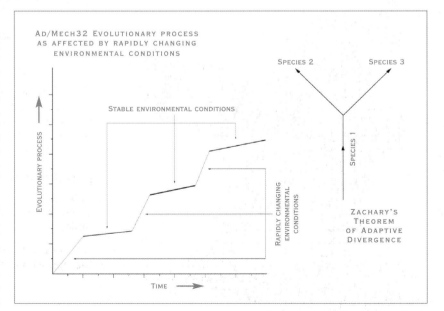

AD/MECH32 EVOLUTIONARY PROCESS AS AFFECTED BY RAPIDLY CHANGING ENVIRONMENTAL CONDITIONS

STABLE ENVIRONMENTAL CONDITIONS

EVOLUTIONARY PROCESS

RAPIDLY CHANGING ENVIRONMENTAL CONDITIONS

TIME

SPECIES 2   SPECIES 3

SPECIES 1

ZACHARY'S THEOREM OF ADAPTIVE DIVERGENCE

TAU SEPTS

A Tau's name contains a great deal of information regarding his place in society, his home world and individual achievements. Following his caste and rank, the third part of a Tau's name is the sept, or system, he hails from. An individual's sept carries a number of subtle meanings and implications regarding the Tau's personality and skills. For example, Tau from one of the elder worlds, the Tau home world or their first colonies, are considered to be erudite and cultured by implication, whereas those from the younger, outlying septs are reckoned to be more vigorous and pragmatic. While these may be considered to be very general traits, there are some worlds or septs which carry more specific meanings, such as T'olku, which is renowned as a centre of administrative training, and many Tau from this world become skilled diplomats and negotiators. The most famous Tau septs and the characteristics commonly associated with them are listed below.

MAJOR SEPTS	COMMONLY ASSOCIATED TRAITS
T'AU	The Tau home world. As the Eldest Sept, Tau from here are considered especially learned and wise.
TAU'N	The first off-world colony of the empire, Tau from this world are considered to be pioneering and often lead exploratory missions throughout Tau space.
VIOR'LA	Vior'la orbits a binary star and translates as 'hot-blooded'. This is a notorious Fire caste world whose warriors are especially aggressive and skilled in the arts of death. The oldest and most respected of the Fire caste academies was founded here many centuries ago.
D'YANOI	Meaning 'twin moons' and isolated for many years from the main body of the Tau empire, the Tau on this world regressed to a more basic level of technology. Though they have since regained their place in the empire, the inhabitants are still regarded as somewhat rustic and backwards.

MAJOR SEPTS	COMMONLY ASSOCIATED TRAITS
DAL'YTH	A very cosmopolitan world where trade is valued as much as conquest. Tau from this world welcome off-worlders and, as such, the world has seen the most contact with alien species. Many Water caste merchants and traders come from this sept.
SA'CEA	One of the hottest and most densely populated Tau worlds, this sept has a greater proportion of Fire warriors than almost any other and is highly militarised. Those hailing from Sa'cea are regarded as particularly disciplined and honourable warriors.
BORK'AN	A centre of learning and academia. with many universities and research facilities. A high percentage of the Fio caste come from this world.
FAL'SHIA	The Fio caste members of this world are famed for the quality of their artisans and their work is much sought after. Many of the most important Tau technological innovations have come from this world, and Tau from this sept are regarded as great problem solvers.

OTHER SEPTS — COMMONLY ASSOCIATED TRAITS

AU'TAAL Well known as a verdant and beautiful sept where those Tau able to move freely throughout the empire may spend their free time relaxing. Tau from this world are known for their easygoing attitude to their duty to the empire and other Tau often regard them as lazy.

ELSY'EIR Renowned for the quantity and quality of their poetry and artwork, Tau from this sept are regarded as intellectuals and are well respected for their creativeness.

KE'LSHAN Situated near the Perdus Rift, this sept has suffered a great deal at the hands of all manner of alien races and, as such, the inhabitants have become mistrustful of those not known to them. These Tau are held to be solemn and taciturn, unfriendly and sometimes openly hostile to alien races.

N'DRAS For reasons unknown, this world was voluntarily abandoned by the Tau nearly half a century ago. The few remaining Tau from N'dras are regarded as being untrustworthy and are generally of quicker temper and brooding countenance.

T'OLKU Known for the sage counsel, debating and diplomatic skills of its Ethereal caste members, many of those Tau who have had successful dealings with alien species originate from this world.

TASH'VAR On the frontier of Tau space, this world has suffered depredations from Orks and other piratical races, and its inhabitants are seen as tenacious and hardy, practical and courageous.

VASH'YA Known as the world 'between spheres', members of the Kor caste have a long tradition on this planet, providing the majority of the pilots and ship crew for the early Tau expansion into space.